Praise for SILENCE

"This book is a breakthrough. In *Silence* Robert Sardello modestly, elegantly—and magisterially—brings thirty years of work in phenomenological, soul-based spiritual psychology to a new level. What was implicit before becomes explicit: spiritual psychology is not just another theory; it is a path to a new reality. Walking it—not just reading, but doing—readers will enter a new creation where all things are made new. Through nine short chapters—each a meditative journey in itself—Sardello phenomenologically unveils silence to be the ground of the world. Each chapter gives practices whereby we can begin to enter into and engage the being of silence ever more deeply and widely, and begin to discover the healing and revelatory wholeness in which we live, move, and exist. This work of the heart is for those who seek the wisdom of the heart for the sake of the heart of the world. Read it and do it!"

—Christopher Bamford
author of *The Voice of the Eagle: The Heart
of Celtic Christianity* and *An Endless Trace:
The Passionate Pursuit of Wisdom in the West*

"Reading Sardello's *Love and the World* was an exciting, heady experience. His book verified and strengthened all I had experienced in eight decades, recharged my faith in life, and brought about a revision of a manuscript I had been immersed in for several years. Sardello's work *Silence* has proved, and is proving to be, quite the opposite. It stopped my world. There was nothing in the work that I could use, extract, or purloin for my purposes. *Silence* stripped me to an embarrassed nakedness that was uncomfortable. From the very beginning of the book, a sharp twinge of an 'anguished longing' long buried within me surfaced, slowed my reading to a snail's pace, and forced me to abandon my usual goal-orientation through which I look at any new writing. The book opens a door within that catches me unaware and anew every time I start reading. I feel quite inadequate to make any statement other than recognizing that this book and its Silence is the key. The key to what, however, I don't know. The work sets a momentum into order every time I pick it up, one which asks only that I stay open to that momentum and drop my ingrained pattern of looking to see where it might lead or "what's in it for me?" I haven't encountered this kind of book before, and I don't know what's in it for me, only that I have a longing to stay open to it. Such a testimonial may be of small use for drawing people to the book—but even purpose of such a noble nature as that seems dishonest in the light of the book itself, and words 'on its behalf' break down. I daresay the work will speak for itself. I can't speak for it except to pray it finds a very wide audience and works its magic thereon."

—Joseph Chilton Pearce
author of *The Biology of Transcendence:*
A Blueprint of the Human Spirit;
Magical Child; and *The Crack in the Cosmic Egg:*
New Constructs of Mind and Reality

About the Author

R obert Sardello, Ph.D., is co-founder with Cheryl Sanders-Sardello, Ph.D., of the School of Spiritual Psychology, which began in 1992. He is author of *Facing the World with Soul, Love and the Soul* (re-issued as *Love and the World*), *Freeing the Soul from Fear,* and *The Power of Soul: Living the Twelve Virtues.* At the University of Dallas, he served as chairman of the Department of Psychology, head of the Institute of Philosophic Studies, and graduate dean. He is also co-founder and faculty member of the Dallas Institute of Humanities and Culture, author of more than 200 articles in scholarly journals and cultural publications, and was on the faculty of the Chalice of Repose Project in Missoula, Montana.

Having developed spiritual psychology based in archetypal psychology, phenomenology, and the Spiritual Science of Rudolf Steiner from over thirty-five years of research in this discipline, as well as holding positions in two universities, he is now an independent teacher and scholar teaching all over the United States, Canada, and the United Kingdom, as well as in the Czech Republic, the Philippines, and Australia. He is a consultant to many educational and cultural institutions, as well as dissertation adviser at numerous academic institutions.

Also by Robert Sardello

Facing the World with Soul

The Power of the Soul:
Living the Twelve Virtues

Freeing the Soul From Fear

Love and the World: A Guide
to Conscious Soul Practice

Love and the Soul

SILENCE

Introduction by Therese Schroeder-Sheker

Reflections by Cheryl Sanders-Sardello

Robert Sardello

nce

The Mystery of Wholeness

GOLDENSTONE PRESS *Benson, North Carolina*

HEAVEN & EARTH PUBLISHING *East Montpelier, Vermont*

NORTH ATLANTIC BOOKS *Berkeley, California*

Published by GOLDENSTONE PRESS, Heaven & Earth Publishing
and North Atlantic Books
P.O. Box 12327
Berkeley, California 94712

Cover photograph and cover design by Susan Quasha
Book design by Factotum, Inc. and Paula Morrison
Printed in the United States of America

Silence: The Mystery of Wholeness is sponsored by the Society for the Study of Native Arts and Sciences, a nonprofit educational corporation whose goals are to develop an educational and cross-cultural perspective linking various scientific, social, and artistic fields; to nurture a holistic view of arts, sciences, humanities, and healing; and to publish and distribute literature on the relationship of mind, body, and nature.

North Atlantic Books' publications are available through most bookstores. For further information, call 800-733-3000 or visit our website at www.northatlanticbooks.com.

Library of Congress Cataloging-in-Publication Data

Sardello, Robert J., 1942–
  Silence : the mystery of wholeness / Robert Sardello.
      p. cm.
  Summary: "Presents ways to achieve self-awareness and access the healing qualities of silence from within"—Provided by North Atlantic Books.
  ISBN 978-1-55643-793-9 (alk. paper)
  1. Silence. 2. Conduct of life. 3. Silence—Religious aspects. 4. Spiritual life. I. Title.
BJ1499.S5S37 2008
248.3'4—dc22

                    2008028789

1 2 3 4 5 6 7 8 9 VERSA 14 13 12 11 10 09 08

For Rose and Albert Sardello,

who live in Silence

TABLE OF CONTENTS

ACKNOWLEDGMENTS

The presence of Silence came some years ago. I first approached saying something of the nature of Silence at several of the Sophia Conferences we at the School of Spiritual Psychology offered yearly. Silence did not come as an idea to elaborate, but as a presence to honor. Cheryl Sanders-Sardello encouraged that work, and added immensely to the understanding of this illusive phenomenon so that it could begin to shine forth. And, she has since then always urged me to be quiet. Encouragement of a very deep nature also came from Therese Schroeder-Sheker, Gail Thomas, Joanne Stroud, Christopher Bamford, Rufus Goodwin, Anne Stockton, Treasa O'Driscoll, Louise Cowan, and Larry Allums. Silence has also been a consistent theme in all of the Sacred Service courses of the School; there are too many people to mention, over one hundred, who have participated and added to developing the capacities for sensing Silence. They each know, though, how grateful I am for what they bring to the work of Spiritual Psychology. I know I risk offending some very helpful people by mentioning only a few, but Janet and John Hampton must be strongly acknowledged, for they are my spiritual mentors.

Then, there is the effort of getting a book done. David Hickman gave his all to get this started and to seeing it through, helping to set up the endeavor of GOLDENSTONE PRESS to do so. I am extremely grateful to Lavon Staveland Ells for incredible editing and proofreading. Our first effort has been elevated to a magnificent level by Gayle Copeland, Tracy Atchley Pentland, and Jim Jacobs, who are responsible for what you are holding in your hands.

INTRODUCTION

by Therese Schroeder-Sheker

The premiere phenomenologist of spiritual psychology comes to us from deep within a Living Silence and, without fanfare, brings to the world a masterpiece of moral imagination. Like an alchemical jeweler, hidden from commerce, Robert Sardello has been pounding and refining gold leaf. He has given the world a work that will undoubtedly become a classic.

At first the lineage of his Silence seems to be a radically pure form of Courtesy, that forgotten, abused, yet vital union of courage, thoughtfulness, and heart that is palpable in the City of God or in the New Jerusalem. This Courtesy is the gesture of Love that fosters the embodiment of intimacy, reverence, and the sacred unity of the three Philosophic Transcendentals—Truth, Beauty, and Goodness. It is as if all five together constellate a circulatory system shaped in the image of the wild rose—five petals, ubiquitous, fragrant, vital, and yet invisible to the curious, the fascinated, or the intrigued.

This unadulterated circulatory system of Courtesy connects Creator and creature, heaven and earth, humans and stars, angels and humans, creatures of all kinds, reverberating from within a new, reorganizing hymn, sacred and timeless. *Ave! Salve!* As the reader proceeds with this five-petalled rose, inside a "text," which is in reality a living, singing well, one slowly but surely awakens to the fact that in the end, in the early part of the twenty-first century, we are holding in our trembling hands a profound theology of incarnation, the significance of which cannot be overlooked or denied, easily summarized or reduced to abstraction. That,

I would venture to say, is the innate and intrinsic power of phenomenology as it comes to expression in the life and lifework of Robert Sardello.

> To find yourself in the infinite,
> You must distinguish and then unite.
> — Goethe [1]

The Silence the author describes is to be entered, not apprehended. With remarkable penetration, quietude, insight, and subtlety, Sardello differentiates between energy and being; emotional attachment and intimacy; separation and autonomy; ego and individuality; the mystery of relating and the psychology of relationship; the invisible and the tangible; an alert, unfocusing focus and trance. He continues to differentiate between the ego-spectator consciousness and witnessing consciousness; experience and concept; incarnational spirituality and out-of-body experience; the living body, and the measurable anatomy and physiology of biomedicine; symptoms and unrecognized possibilities; image-consciousness and either fantasy or outward perceiving. This calm, concentrated sifting proceeds to its and thous; appearances and realities; perceptions and preconceptions; entities and individuating aspects; emotion and feeling; reaction and responsivity; passion and freedom; guilt and contrition. Do you understand? This is not "merely" a labor of love and a work of discernment (though those would be a blessing). Nor is this capacity to differentiate either an analysis (where we are then left with disassembled parts and no whole) or a formal disputatio.

One finds great rest in these pages. Sardello's capacity for differentiation consistently stands as the requisite prelude to the alchemical reunion, the conjunction of opposites. As with the phenomena of sound,[2] the more highly differentiated and nuanced the pitch experiences are the greater the structure and eventual possibility of repose. Amazingly, this rest or repose is described on the penultimate page as comfort, the presence of the

Comforter, an English name we use to describe the Paraclete. The Latin word *paracleta* means "the one who answers the cry." This living, billowing Silence is needed to be able to hear the cry of the soul, and the cry is needed in order for the Comforter to respond. This is a work of great importance and is filled with the breath of the Holy Spirit.

Along the way, as if bridging each chapter, linking one to another, Cheryl Sanders-Sardello writes antiphonally and experientially in the unmistakable voice of a poet of rare sensibility. Her bridge pieces are love letters or hymns, placed ever so quietly on an invisible altar we readers are allowed to approach. A rhythm ensouls this work: chapter and hymn, or, if we evoke Bach, prelude and fugue. Either way, it is a beautiful rhythm that models the very inner work that Robert Sardello brings to the fore.

In nine increasingly deep corridors of an interior journey, Sardello describes how, in the sacramental dynamism of Silence, a new capacity for soul-spirit consciousness allows us to anticipate the world as holy, and in this transformed world, new life is continually coming into being and is perceived as if within liturgy. Urgency abounds, yet without fear, perhaps because heart resonance is sovereign in Silence, prompting the mystery of true prayer. As important, the life of prayer, midwifed through Silence, allows us to experience spiritual presences right here amidst daily life.

A number of years ago, Hans Urs von Balthasar[3] pointed out that Georges Bernanos, that enormously creative French writer and physician of the soul, once described sin as that patterned way of being in which we remain living at the surface. Dear Friends, make no mistake: Robert Sardello is asking us to abandon surface impressions and patterns, to abandon what has become comfortable, and to embrace a sacred depth of being that asks us to enter that which is wholly unknown and that which fosters genuine metanoia. By extension, he says, this Holy Silence makes possible a life of prayer, in service of that which is far greater than our mere selves, at the same time it creates an inner clearing for the human being.

This life-renewing Silence heals the ambitious, self-serving, and often cruel goal of self-improvement, and reveals instead the activity of spiritual beings and spiritual life. In this realm, there are neither extremes of clever abstraction nor passion-charged emotion, which so convincingly simulates life, replacing hot intensity or cool clarity for authenticity. In actuality, these consumptive currents become forces of death, not life, in that continual upheaval is followed by depletion. This depletion is not to be confused, for example, with the Christian practice of inner emptiness, or kenosis, an inner clearing that makes room for new life, including living, breathing Silence. This is not to say that the clearing or releasing can occur without sorrow or loss. However, light appears where there was formerly "no room in the inn." In this dimension where time has become space, life is renewed and enlivened. But beware of the agnostic reflex, our brave author commands us! "Blocking the light of the soul results in a further need to attach to prepackaged things, ideas, and emotions, because they provide a semblance of light. When light is blocked, we develop a desire for things, not for Silence."

Throughout each of the nine chapters, Sardello provides the reader with profound exercises relating to each phase of Silence, so that we may participate in, rather than follow or parrot, a great phenomenologist's work. In this way, he ceaselessly advocates the necessity of personal responsibility and the holiness of freedom, encouraging one and all, in whatever their capacity or condition, to the necessity of inner work. Assent and service going hand in hand in Silence, we enter that which is wholly unknown with a creative purity that is startling, precisely because we are accompanied by the presence of the Third, or the companion-presence: Love. The role of grace in Silence and companioning is deeply developed, as is modesty, but in far-reaching human and spiritual terms, wrung from new life rather than an earlier, though honorable and more familiar, framework.

Be that as it may, it became impossible for me to read this book without recognizing in the author a profoundly Christian voice and a Christianizing destiny. There is no proselytizing. There is no hidden agenda. It is startling: he does not call upon the name of God, nor does he situate himself in the cultural space of a religion. He does not seek our conversion to or alignment with an institution. (During the course of the book, he refers to such diverse traditions as Pythagoreans and Sufis, Henry Corbin and Jacob Lorber.) Yet by the time I had reached the end of the seventh chapter, I had begun to wonder if the author hadn't had an unspoken Moses-by-the-Burning-Bush experience, and if, in the limitless Love of that nonconsuming fire, this burning, radiant, urgent Silence emerged for him as a hidden name for Christ. You could say that is my projection or interpretation, and this would be fair, save for an undeniable motion on the part of the author, who is always moving towards an altar hidden from view.

As if in immediate response to my inner question, the eighth and ninth crowning chapters appear in voice and gesture as unmistakably feminine and Marian. Through the agency of an embodied modesty that is simultaneously humble and noble, the author describes a kind of spiritual activity in which the human heart is the mystical yet literal vessel of pregnancy. Here, Sardello differentiates between spirituality of the heart and the heart's spirituality; one partakes, and the other cocreates and is inwardly radiating. The cocreating bears the imprint of a remarkable trinity of activities that characterizes Holy Silence: service, healing, and worship. Through devotion and reverence in the innermost chamber of the heart, the author describes the Holy Silence that generates the experience of a Divine Being who protects the mystery of freedom and calls us to awaken. He then continues and differentiates between psychological projection, with which many are already familiar, and the projection of inner alchemy, in which the culminating transformation projects outward. Whatever the projection touches transmutes to gold. Or, echoing the earlier intuitions of the five-petalled circulatory system, rose gold.

All the previous chapters seem to be headed toward not merely human transformation but the transubstantiation of the world. Sardello is saying that Holy Silence is calling us to bring the entirety of our human experiences and perceptions to and through a hidden altar, deep within the human body and heart, for the good of the world. This is a theology of incarnation and is profoundly Eucharistic, though our author would never present himself as a theologian. There was a time, in the desert tradition so long ago, when the word *theologian* was understood to refer to a person who personally knew God, was in relationship with God, not someone who was able to speak or write *about* God or had the ability to describe with startling acuity (love and artistry) the depth of religious thought. My impression is that Sardello began as a psychologist, emerged as a phenomenologist of spiritual psychology, and now, in the fullness of voice that reflects the concentration of decades of prayer and contemplation, he stands, however unexpectedly, as a theologian as well, in the oldest and most beautiful sense of the word.

By the time we reach the crowning chapter nine, the author brings us openly into Silence as the foundation of prayer and, by extension, the relationships that are possible with spiritual beings. Here, he names the possibility of an angel, a saint, Christ, or Mary. A uniquely Christian gift to human spirituality affirms that we can have a personal relationship with God. Our God is not simply a cosmic, impersonal energy pulsating though the universe, though for Christians, the Risen Christ affects all of life, and for Jews, to pray is to be heard, and to converse with the Master of the Universe. Here, Sardello gifts the entire theocentric spiritual community (Jews, Christians, and more) when he declares that praying within Holy Silence has specific qualities. Foremost, he says, the words do not evoke images but become like images, in that we can experience the very words themselves as if they were spreading out into space, like the formation of crystals on a window in winter. This is when the words etch or engrave themselves, as the psalms say, on the heart and remain the ground of being.

Prayer is a creative act. Perhaps without ever meaning to, Sardello makes a Johan-nine spirituality palpable. Unashamed to stand vigil with the truly feminine and rooted within the unity of matter and spirit-Word made flesh, he extends, like John, tender goodness, beauty, and truth into the world and notes that this orientation to prayer also transforms our daily speech. Soon, prayer moves out of or sacrifices any tendency to self-centered request, and in that it reflects true conversation (listening and responding) creates an entirely new world.

The culminating book in the Bible is a book of revelation and describes a new Heaven and a new Earth created out of this very condition of prayer, the communion between the two worlds. The love that is magnified in this prayerful circulatory system, from Earth to Heaven and back again, will transform the physical world and even the universe. Thus, prayer is not something we do for ourselves, nor is it something one does alone, but it is something we do as a community of spiritual beings whose very existence must be that of praying. This theology of embodiment, of the unified body, soul, and spirit, and, by extension, the offering of self in service to the Divine, which is so intrinsically Eucharistic, has emerged from the author following a sustained meditation on Holy Silence that culminates in prayer. This is a lifetime work, not a thesis, not an abstraction.

Somehow, it is not possible for me to lay down this exquisite work or to hold such pages in my hands without reflecting on an echo or a resonance. I hear it in my heart. Only sixty-five years ago, the Jewish philosopher Edith Stein, one of the greatest phenomenologists of the twentieth century, wrote quietly and persistently along similar veins, ways, and means. Organically, she had gradually moved from psychology to philosophy, and eventually her relentless quest for truth became the purest theology.[4] It is well-known that her philosophical-theological writings began with empathy and eventually were concerned with the nature and structure of the human person, composed of body, soul, and spirit. She perceived things in their originality, and through calm, penetrating sense-perception, devoted years to the phenomenology of body, soul, and spirit. With time, she entered Holy Silence and the Living Word so deeply that her prayer life asked new and unexpected things of her, things of an ultimate and sacrificial nature. Because interior prayer and exterior action were inseparable for her, Stein made her solemn profession as a Carmelite nun in 1938. In short order she was arrested by the Nazis in 1942 and days later died a voluntary martyr in the concentration camp at Auschwitz.

The entire Judeo-Christian world knows of her powerful life and death, and one cannot deny that the mystery of her death overshadowed her philosophical legacy of phenomenology. It is critical to honor a life freely given. Perhaps, too, it has taken us decades to regain some sort of equilibrium following the absolute cacophony of genocide, during which her great written work has admittedly paled in light of Auschwitz. Phenomenology itself requires years of quiet observer-participant reflection, and, in a specific way, Edith Stein was silenced.

It is not insignificant then that Robert Sardello echoes a certain strand from a Christian phenomenology and begins anew in the very Silence that was overlooked in the decades of postwar chaos. All interiority involves a deep relationship to Silence, and this particular work appears, with perfect timing, at a time when collective emotional noise is almost deafening. This is a book unlike any other. It is easy to see that the discipline of phenomenology, so richly, beautifully, and penetratingly developed as a sustained meditation, calls new and profound capacities into existence. These capacities, when turned toward spirituality, teach a methodology that allows people from many walks of life to participate in rather than talk about the deepening relationship with God. Furthermore, this level of interiority links freedom and responsibility in ways that are vital.

But the movement from psychology to phenomenological theology, as demonstrated in this slender volume, calls for a radical receptivity united to practical application. Together, as Sardello's vision so beautifully sings, these create a foundation for service, healing, and worship in a time when our institutional forms are imploding. Though we humans suffer in times of confusion and transition, it is said that our implosions, inner and outer, must occur in order for that which is truly new and living to emerge. Furthermore, every birth entails the confluence of past, present, and future, and somehow it is right that service, healing, and worship constellate a trinity wherein time becomes space.

In that light, and on this Thanksgiving day, one can only laud Robert Sardello's quietude, pray that people all over the world find this book, and that they respond again, as once before, to the call of Silence, the voice of Eternity.

—Therese Schroeder-Sheker
The Chalice of Repose Project
Mt. Angel, Oregon
Thanksgiving 2005

[1] J. W. von Goethe (1749–1832), excerpt from *Atmosphere*

[2] See this illustrated in Hans Jenny's *Cymatics* (Newmarket, NH: Macromedia, 2001).

[3] Hans Urs von Balthasar, *Bernanos: An Ecclesial Existence*. (San Francisco: Ignatius Press, 1996).

[4] Edith Stein (Sr. Teresa Benedicta of the Cross) lived from 1891 to 1942 and was canonized a saint in 1998. See Waltraud Herbstrith's *Edith Stein*. 2nd ed. (San Francisco: Ignatius Press, 1992).

An Entry

All spiritual traditions value Silence. *The Tao Te Ching* speaks of the Tao as "for lack of a better word, the Great Way. It flows, circles, flows and circles. And it has no name." So described, the Tao is probably the same as Silence, for the currents of Silence that I describe in this book are within this kind of imagination. Meister Eckhart says this of Silence: "The central silence is the purest element of the soul, the soul's most exalted place, the core, the essence of the soul." Here, the exalted place of Silence as constitutive of soul correlates with all that this book says concerning a new manner of living the great inner life. Pythagoras said, "Learn to be silent. Let your quiet mind listen and absorb the silence." Silence is autonomous. It is beyond us; our task is to coordinate our being with the greater Being of Silence.

The traditions have always recognized the autonomy of Silence. Silence is not something that we do, nor is it a personal capacity. We can become quiet and by doing so the door to Silence opens. Krishnamurti agrees: "This quietness, this silence is the highest form of intelligence which is never personal, never yours or mine. Being anonymous, it is whole and immaculate." Lao Tsu speaks of Silence: "The ten thousand things rise and fall while the Self watches their return. They grow and flourish and then return to the source. Returning to the source is Silence, which is the way of nature." Here, what is spoken of as the Self corresponds with what in this writing we speak of as the capacity of attention necessary to find and be conscious with the Silence. Of the many things Rumi says of Silence, here is one: "Sit quietly, and listen for a voice that will say, Be more silent."

What, then, can we add to Silence in this writing? Would it not be of more benefit to go on a silent retreat, visit a monastery, read the masters of the religious traditions? Doing any of these things would not be nearly as complex as trying to follow the threads of this book or, even more, taking up the suggested practices. This more complex way is suggested because, while everything the religious and spiritual traditions say concerning Silence is both beautiful and true, it is no longer possible for us to get to Silence in those ways, not in ways that bridge the gap between Silence and the noisy world. Maybe if we leave the noisy world behind and become a monk, it is still possible to enter Silence through the religious tradition. And it is entirely possible to enter deeply into Silence during a retreat or a religious ritual, but when we leave, we leave it behind, except as a sweet memory. This writing offers a new way of thinking about Silence. It also presents practical, realistic ways in which we can come to feel-sense the subtle activity occurring within the realm of Silence. There, within it, we can come to experience more fully this highest form of intelligence wherein "the ten thousand things rise and fall while the Self watches their return."

An understandable tendency exists to evoke the realms of Silence while essentially remaining outside of them. This approach has the advantage of producing an emotional identification with Silence, a false feeling of participation, without the careful meditative work needed to reorient our lives to be in constant resonance with the Silence. Most writing on Silence follows this direction, quoting the religious traditions and extolling the personal benefits of solitude, which is actually something quite different than encountering the worlds of Silence. Recognizing this tendency, this writing concentrates instead on doing and making available the strong descriptive work necessary for anyone to start anew with Silence and discover for oneself what Silence provides. Among the things learned is the way out of the confines of the oppressive nature of our egotism, which takes innumerable forms, the most impressive being that of acting as if one's religious demeanor, acquired by reading and even studying what the mystics have experienced and the theologians have theorized about, qualifies one as a lover of Silence.

A more descriptive and phenomenological approach to Silence is necessary in our time, for we not only have to rediscover lost realms, but also, at the same time, clear away our deeply ingrained desire to live by what others have said rather than discover inner truths for ourselves. In promoting this latter approach to the inner life, I follow the inspiration of the spiritual science of Rudolf Steiner, Anthroposophy. However, here too, an important difference has to be stated, for otherwise we land right back in the center of the same kind of living off the fruits of the thoughts of others we are seeking to escape. This writing works anthroposophically; that is, it is careful research into an aspect of the inner life, done in such a way that anyone can verify what is stated by simply doing the inner work. This writing is not a work of anthroposophy in the sense of following what the master has already put forth and is already available.

This book is offered to you as an experience that deepens your relationship with the world and all that is within it. But it is offered as an experience of Silence, not as information, and to receive it requires attending to your interior feeling while reading. If you read this book only for information with the thought that you will see the imagery and experience the movement of Silence later, "when you have time," you will have missed entering into developing the capacities to do so. This writing is not

3

only about Silence; it is a speaking that resonates from the Silence. Reading the text in the most helpful way requires a willingness to put aside boundaries set by the clock and step outside the conceptual boundaries imposed by our common culture. So I suggest you read it over time, in the way of a meditative practice. You will then be inviting the subtleties of Silence to unfold within you in such a manner that you will begin to notice these qualities in the world.

It is less helpful to read *about* Silence than it is to find ways of entering into it. There are a number of practices in this book that assist experiencing Silence as a whole and also many different dimensions of the Silence. Nearly all of these practices come from a course, *Sacred Service,* offered by the School of Spiritual Psychology. Cheryl Sanders-Sardello and I, with the assistance of others, have taught this course for the past five years, so the practices have been tried, refined, and validated as not only completely safe but also life-altering. These practices are something more than technical instructions on how to be with the Silence. They are better seen as *spiritual manners,* ways of behaving that invite the spiritual presence of Silence into our lives and reorient our lives to be in service to the spiritual worlds.

A practice differs considerably from an exercise or a technique. A practice intends to develop new capacities by developing dimensions of attention and objects of attention that go beyond usual forms of consciousness. An exercise such as group work may, under certain conditions, produce a momentary experience of a new dimension, but there will not be enough inner strength of will to continue to experience that dimension. And techniques tend to be manipulative, often attempting to make something happen rather than helping others to discover what lies within their own abilities. The whole of this book is a practice. If you read carefully and thoughtfully and relinquish running after information, you will be well on the way toward the formation of new capacities.

A significant alteration of your consciousness will take place. Any of the stated practices are no more than particular points of emphasis that help you to slow down and stay within the process that the writing takes you through.

THE ENORMITY OF LIFE'S *tasks weigh and press on the day . . . they demand and insist on a constancy of attention that is relentless. Ah . . . but we are fortunate to have night's solace—in the silence that is created by the dark.*

Night . . . that melancholy time, when the stars remind us of the silence of God. Here we can remember the future, and lean into the unknown, setting aside the oppressive weight of our carefully constructed version of who we think we are, and release that side of the pool. We can remember how to see in the dark . . . with our ears . . . perceiving the silence in its holy echoing and resonance, its calling forth a knowing that is from the soul.

This silence sends us on a different pilgrimage. It guards the heart's fire and teaches us to speak from within, with a language that is imbued with the sacred. Words thus nurtured in this holy silence fly forth with the wings of joy, and return to lead us back to the silence from which they were born.

— Cheryl Sanders-Sardello

CHAPTER I

A Meditation on Silence

Each of us has an ever-faithful companion-presence. Something that is always with us. Something that helps us to live with inner integrity and depth, to see through the outer coverings of others and of the world to their purpose and core being, and to get over placing ourselves at the center of everything. This companion-presence is Silence. It never goes away. We go away from it, become distracted and forgetful, and lose the manners needed to nurture companionship with it. We go away from Silence into the world of noise as if into a vast buzzing of insects, pushed to exist within the permanent irritation of dissonance.

Our choosing to live in the noise of our thoughts and emotions—within the incessant clamor around us—happens almost without our recognition. But we are uncomfortable with the Silence. It does not go with our hectic lives, with what must be done every day, and with our felt need to accomplish something. Moments of quiet remind us that we have neglected the core of our being, and we cannot face the implications of this neglect. Anxiety enters. It's better to keep running away from it.

What are we running from? We have a strong tendency to imagine Silence as the absence of sound. This imagination deprives Silence of being anything in itself and makes it an emptiness, a void in what should be the norm. But Silence was here before anything else, and it envelops everything else. It is the most primary phenomenon of existence, both palpably something and seemingly nothing. Silence is prior to sound, not the cessation of sound. It is already present. If we drop into quietness for just a moment, we feel the presence of Silence as an invitation.

The center of our bodily being is the organ for receiving this invitation from the Silence. As we enter the mystery of Silence, its presence resonates throughout the fibers of our flesh, while extending beyond the flesh to the soul inwardly and to the cosmos outwardly. Our body's center is the necessary meeting point where the inward silence of solitude meets up with the great Silence of Cosmic Wisdom. When we do not cultivate this meeting point in the right ways, we lose access to our soul, to the presence of the Silence, and to our individual place in the Wisdom of the World. Without Silence, we are lost and cannot get still enough to find our way back.

Silence bears the wholeness we keep looking for while we do not know exactly what we are looking for. It is around us and within us. It goes to the deepest depths of the soul and to the outermost reaches of the cosmos and continually unites the two at the centering place of our heart. Here we discover the power of re-creation. Here everything comes alive again as if for the first time. This secret and this mystery are so revolutionary that all who aspire to commercialize the world conspire to bury this secret in the noise of the world. And the intimation of the strength of this mystery causes us to run to that noise, though we are not conscious that we are doing so.

Great bewilderment exists about the impetus to find our soul and our place in the world when confusion exists around this phenomenon of Silence. Because there are forces promoting this confusion with all their resources, we can no longer take it for granted. Happiness and

Silence belong together just as do profit and noise. So long as we live in a commercialized world, noise reigns. All the distractions that keep us from the center of our being, where stillness of soul can resonate with Silence, belong to the world of profit.

We think that our respite from this "unacknowledged conspiracy" against the healing power of Silence can be found in nature, for that is where we first go in search of stillness. There is an affinity between the natural world and Silence. Silence envelops nature and gathers nature to her as a blessed place of intensity. Nonetheless, what is available in nature is available everywhere, if we but learn how to attract it properly. All religious traditions, all forms of meditation, and all rituals attract Silence. Yet strangely, users of these traditions acknowledge Silence mostly as a starting point to launch into whatever they each promote. Hurling toward their goals in their multitude of ways, they do not realize that they have reached it with their very first step. They are unaware that it is necessary to develop the inner discipline of disclosing what is present, rather than setting out on a path looking for something somewhere else.

Naming the personal benefits of Silence is easy. We feel a new sense of freedom and a capacity to be ourselves again. We may be shocked to notice that we had not even realized we had lost ourselves. We feel a new attunement to spirit as a directly felt reality. We gain the capacity of reflection, of letting the world and things and others mirror within us, rather than ceaselessly going from one activity to the next. We realize that our activity had become an addiction. We gain a newfound creativity. Insights, new ideas, and new ways of seeing come again. But all these results are by-products of Silence and not reasons for becoming intrigued with it. To prematurely focus on its gifts—to ask what this experience will do for me—severely limits how deep we are able to go into the Silence, and makes us complacent and satisfied with mere imitations of the phenomenon.

Silence knows how to hide. It gives a little and waits to see what we do. When we take what is offered to use for our own purposes, it goes into obscurity. Some of us are content with the little we receive and devise all sorts of ways to return to that simple, first offering: A day in the woods. Fishing. Music. A walk on the beach. A trek in the mountains. A vacation. Even this first offering is inexhaustible, for this limited way has no boundary. However, because we think we stumble into Silence by leaving the world of chaos behind for a time, a gap separates the world of noise from the world of Silence. It feels as if there is no way over that gap. We feel that we are either consumed by the clatter of the world or else totally embraced, for a few moments, by the arms of Silence. The two remain separate, with clatter getting most of the attention. In fact, we come to the point of needing the noise, while we can stand only the smallest doses of repose. This situation is a terrible reversal of what is required to live a healthy life.

We think we can find Silence by being quiet for a while, going inward, getting back in touch with ourselves, disengaging for a time from all of the pressures and tensions of life. This limited view is like getting to the door of a cathedral and thinking that is the whole of the experience. We do feel better under such circumstances because we are returned to ourselves, a necessary condition for the reception of this mystery. The fuller part of the experience, however, is what we feel around us and what touches us. We have a bodily perception of being welcomed into the vastness and fecundity of Silence, and the world appears to change radically as it attends that welcoming. When we find the entry into this large stillness, our lives are irrevocably changed because at that moment a monumental transition takes place: we find that the center of the universe shifts from our self-interests, even our spiritual self-interests, to the larger world, even to the cosmos, which we now begin to perceive as a spiritual reality.

Our newly discovered engagement with the larger world persists. It does not become just another passing interest, because the experience comes with astonishing intimacy and feels like the finding of a long lost beloved. Before we entered the Silence, no gentleness existed between our soul and the world, our soul and the divine, or our soul and others. We implicitly had thought the world to be harsh, filled with fear, a constant struggle. We were living in a state of disease and never recognized it. The only symptom was a constant inner longing for something, and we did not know what it was.

Silence is palpable. It is a kind of subtle substance, which we can almost reach out to feel. And yet it is not there around us unless it is also here within us. It has favorite gathering places, such as the natural world, a forest, the mountains, the empty plains; the outback is thick with it. Other places of subtle congregation are cathedrals, caves, sacred sites, and cemeteries. In meditation we run into it at the moment when our interior becomes a vast exterior, and we no longer know if we are inside or outside. Sometimes it gathers between human beings. It presents itself at births, at deaths, and at most religious ceremonies. It sometimes comes when we pray. The religion of the Quakers is founded on it. But it requires going to the edge of selflessness before it will appear, so religion itself does not guarantee its presence.

These places of gathering are fast disappearing. A friend in Japan recently told me that one Sunday he went on a train to the mountains to get away from the press of people in the city. As he was walking in the woods, he suddenly heard a loud beep. He looked up and saw a loudspeaker attached to a tree. A long announcement suddenly blared through the speaker. The Silence fled immediately. We are not yet quite in that situation in this country. It is still possible to seek Silence in nature. But cathedrals are less quiet than in the past. Religious ceremonies are completely prefabricated to ensure the numinous stays away, and we take only a "moment of silence" to remember the dead. Caves and sacred sites and art museums are insulated from this mystery by guided tours filled with the noise of information. We now have to learn to invite the Silence, and having invited it, we now have to learn to enter it.

In our ordinary sensing, perceiving, and thinking, everything around us exists as "outside" and "over there." We are spectators to ourselves and to the world. But in Silence everything displays its depth, and we find that we are part of the depth of everything around us. We are not adding our subjectivity to the world but discovering that the kind of separation between ourselves and the world we have adopted is illusion. We do not dissolve into the world, nor does the world dissolve into us in Silence; we and the world each mirror the other within the depths of the soul. We discover that each thing of the world lives deeply within us. But more, we discover that each of us, in the region of the soul, lives deeply within the soul of the world and the crossing point is the centering heart.

Drawing attention to the heart focuses the mystery we are entering. As both physical organ and spiritual-imaginative center, the heart is the only true organ for perceiving Silence. Once activated in the heart, Silence spreads throughout the body, and we feel as if our entire physiology alters. Instead of perceiving things held apart from other things in sharp and heavy outline, as is usual, we enter into a feeling-perception of the interior space around us that gives birth to all things. Artists have an intuition of this kind of interior in working with negative space. But the space of Silence is something more than that because it is not merely the void from which things spring up; it is a living presence. The deeper we enter into Silence the more we become aware that this living presence is primary, and the contents of our perceiving are the secondary bursting forth of this original presence. For a moment we are dizzied beyond belief. If only we had the courage to ward off the dizziness and stay in its presence, who knows where we would be taken. Instead, we recover our usual sensing and, at most, feel the continued resonance of the Silence.

We can learn, however, to cultivate the feeling of resonance so that it becomes an indicator that lets us know when we are near the gateway to the interior world of Silence. The word *resonance* comes from the Latin verb *resonare*, meaning "to return to sound." When we sound an object such as a bell, it continues to ring or resonate the original sound. There is another kind of resonance called *sympathetic resonance:* when a bell sounds and continues to resonate, another object with qualities of the same pitch as the bell begins to vibrate with it. The human soul functions similarly as an activity of resonance, and our soul connection with Silence is a form of sympathetic resonance, though it is an inverse resonance because it is not the sound that resonates but the currents of Silence.

When we cultivate the capacity to be alone without feeling lonely, we enter into solitude where we find ourselves anew. Solitude, however, too easily turns into spiritual narcissism. It is like the single bell resonating only its own sound. We become filled with ourselves, imagining that we are in the presence of the larger world of Silence. Yet *sympathetic resonance,* a term that comes from the world of physics, is not quite descriptive for getting beyond ourselves. Perhaps it is better understood as requiring *empathetic resonance,* the resonance of the individual soul coming into resonance with the Soul of the World.

In Silence, everything is experienced as "within" but not as "within us." We, along with everything else, are within Silence. Here new laws of perceiving hold. In our ordinary sensing and perceiving, we experience things as outside of us, in front of us, to the side of us, above, below, and behind us. The physical body limits our perspectives. When we perceive something while we are in the realm of Silence, we perceive qualities of the interior of things from the place of our own interior being. For example, in ordinary perceiving, the tree that sits outside a window is "over there." As long as we perceive it as "over there," we are not present to the Silence. From within Silence, the boundary between us and the tree becomes a diaphanous substance. We are then taken out of the kind of perceiving that knows in advance what it perceives into a way that is present to the unknown. Here, feeling ascends—not emotion, but feeling. It is a new way of knowing, knowing as artists or musicians know when practicing their art.

At the exact moment we shift from mental knowing into perceiving presence, the thing we are perceiving through Silence glows as something living and autonomous even if it is an "inanimate" thing. Is this new perceiving merely a projection of our psyche? Are the qualities we perceive mere unconscious and subjective feelings that we are not aware of until we project them? An answer depends on how alert we are. Projecting is a distinct possibility. It happens if we do not know how to enter the realm of feeling while remaining in the sphere of clarity, so it is important that we know how to distinguish between projecting something from within our soul and an objective perceiving of the Silence. The difference is that when we are projecting we are unaware of our participation in what we experience. It is as if our perception is completely separate from us. When we perceive the world wrapped in Silence, we are very aware of being within a consciousness very different from spectator consciousness. The Silence we perceive is as much in us as within whatever we are perceiving. We have overcome dualistic consciousness.

Each time we venture into the realm of Silence consciously, not merely by accident, our soul is strengthened and a feeling-with-clarity emerges. When we become just a bit more alert within this realm, we discover something paradoxical. This realm of Silence is filled with currents of activity. We do not enter into loneliness or isolation but into the deepest feeling of communing. Our soul feels full, whole, and completely within its own milieu. The soul finds spirit-beings of its own kind here.

We cannot perceive these others directly, but it is still clear to us that active presences are here, and any sense we may have of being alone completely dissolves. Indeed, each thing in our world seems to be a mirror or a counterpart of one or more of these active presences. Each thing we perceive in Silence shines forth with new clarity and integrity. The unseen presences mirror themselves within things, but they do not narrow themselves to the confines of those things. If we enter Silence by way of meditation, we find these presences, and when we focus on them, they seem to be throughout our body. We experience them as a healing activity that continues as long as we are able to stay within that realm. When in meditation we move on to focus on some thought or image, these beings of the Silence surround the thought or image, becoming its milieu. What sets apart the realm of Silence from other experiences that typically occur in meditation is that the world is not left behind. No. Right here, within this world, we discover immediate evidence of invisible worlds by taking up the physics of engagement with what cannot be seen but is so strongly felt as to give us certainty.

Everything, it seems, has its own quality of silence. It is a unified but many-qualitied phenomenon. The Silence of high, rocky mountains can be felt as an immensity of Silence that contacts us in such a way that we feel ourselves as one with its immensity, its immovability, and its vastness. In such moments, these spiritual qualities are alive and animated. A dense forest has another kind of Silence. It's darker, deeper, and more inward; we feel our experience much more from within our body. There are also the happy silences of the wandering stream, the radiant but oppressive silence of the pyramids, the magical silence of the stars casting spells over the whole of the earth, the vast interior silence of the cathedral whose walls seem built around the silence, and the silence of a leaf falling into the Silence that enfolds it. We can imagine assembling a vast catalogue of such qualities of Silence.

The great Silence of the sky stretches over all silences; beneath all silences lies the great Silence of the earth. Waves of quiet move between the silences as intertwining currents. The soul of each creature, each thing, and each being unites with these currents. It is as if each thing, in its particularity, arises out of and is sustained by this interplay, giving subtle form and diverse qualities of silence to what otherwise would be too vast for any mortal to perceive.

YES, JUST THERE, *I can step outside and be inside the comfort of you—walking into the arms of protection, the embrace of safety. You wait there for me; there is never any doubt you are there. Chaos can enter my mind; many alien forms can cloud my heart. Yet since I was very young I have known that in this place of yours I can be refound, renewed, re-formed.*

Knowing I can go there has always helped, but it has never made the pain less, just less powerful. At first it seemed I could hear you, present faintly in the vacuous, empty whole. Later I knew I was hearing your touch, and from the place of infinite connections, I was hearing all that is said without words. When no one speaks, the possibility that all that has ever been spoken to be heard becomes magnified. Even when what has not been said is the most profound, I still hear the summoning of all silence and come quickly to be counted among the devoted.

Shhhhh…, we cannot hear the silence when all are trying to lay claim to her treasure; when so few are concerned for her extinction. She is like the hole in the ozone, global warming, and the plight of the frogs. We do not believe the danger is real. We do not trust there is anything there to lose. Is there? Of course there is. It is the only way left to us.

— Cheryl Sanders-Sardello

CHAPTER 2

The Guardians of Silence

Silence is the bountiful source of our sensing our self and all creation with newfound clarity and intimacy. Why, then, don't we all just be quiet? The noisiness of our thoughts and feelings and images, as well as the outer world of anti-silence, keeps us from even getting close to the boundary of this realm. Should we try to get close we run into anxiety, dread, fear, temptation, distraction, fantasy, and even the peculiar feeling of being attacked. Henri Nouwen calls Silence "the furnace of transformation." Ah, here's the problem... and the challenge. We cannot just find and enjoy silence. We cannot simply add it on to whoever we are as if it were a new commodity. It thoroughly changes us. Forever. So we flirt with it, but we hold back from becoming its servant. Avoiding Silence, we avoid transforming from oppressive enmeshment with ourselves and with attendant matters of the world into spiritual servants.

There are two ways we can look at the many distracting forces that keep us from Silence. One way is to see them as they have been seen in the spiritual tradition—as beings that intend to pull us into chaos and earthly desires and to trap us in our own egotism. The other way is to see these same forces as guardians of the realm of Silence, as beings that intend to keep us from wandering into Silence without the inner soul work needed to ensure that we do not use this experience for our egotistic needs.

The first way is based on a theology that leads us to divide the universe into two parts, good and bad. Our task is not theological; it is more descriptive. It attempts to present what happens inwardly as we approach Silence. We can re-read the tradition of the guardians in this light.

Until we develop an inner discipline within our soul, we feel rebuffed, turned away, and cast aside when we try to enter the Silence in a conscious way and go deeply into it. If our soul does not go through a time of preparation and purification, which may be a long time, we will form no capacity to enter and explore the intricacies of this landscape. Without inner work on our part, Silence seems to be an unformed, dark, mysterious realm without specification of any kind. In such vague space, we desire only to receive a sense of wholeness that this inner experience offers. We desire it for our own personal enhancement. However, there is much more to this realm than the rippling after-image of feeling "whole," a feeling we mistake for the essence of the experience.

Our soul is not to be regarded as a higher—as distinct from a lower—self but as a vibrating link through which our human personality perceives the influences exerted by the cosmos. At the same time, our soul is equally a link to every earthly desire. Left on its own, soul gravitates toward earthly desires and becomes forgetful of its connection with the spiritual cosmos. Silence is the primary means by which this connection can be reestablished and desire can be turned again toward the stars, without abandoning the world. We would expect, then, that spirit beings would gather at the threshold where Silence also gathers to make sure that we do not simply transfer our earthly desires to the spiritual domains. That kind of transference results in our being attracted to the spiritual realms as if they offered essentially the same kind of pleasures and experiences as any other of our desires. A dire mistake.

St. Anthony, the Christian Desert Father of the third and fourth century who is credited with establishing monastic life, can be considered an initiate into the realm of Silence. An initiate is someone who ventures into the cosmic worlds and brings a new spiritual impulse that is intended for all of humanity. The initiate then lives this impulse, showing the way. Due to St. Anthony and the other Desert Fathers, spiritual Silence was introduced into the earthly plane. He spent twenty years alone in the desert, making a way for the rest of humanity to find Silence more easily should it so choose. His biographer, St. Athanasius, describes the bouts Anthony had with the guardian:

> He [the guardian of Silence] advanced against the youth, noisily disturbing him by night and so troubling him in the daytime that those who watched were aware of the bouts that occupied them both. The one hurled foul thought and the other overturned them through his prayers.... [T]he beleaguered devil undertook one night to assume the form of a woman and to imitate her every gesture, solely in order that he might beguile Anthony. But in thinking about the Christ and considering the excellence won through him, and the intellectual part of the soul, Anthony extinguished the fire of his opponent's deception. (from Athanasius, *The Life of St. Anthony*)

The guardians of this threshold preside over the border between our soul's attraction to physical experience in the physical world and our soul's longing for something unknown but familiar, the homeland of the soul. We are attracted to Silence but then quickly become bored with it and find ourselves equally attracted to the glamour of the world. We do not see it, but when we try to enter this region without preparation and we are summarily thrown back across the borderland, this is the work of the guardians.

Something important happens here, even before we encounter the guardians, for these guardians surround us always; they do not suddenly appear only when we search for quietude. The very moment we still ourselves and become aware of our inner life we abandon all of our moorings in the world—our well-known identity, our past, our thoughts, hopes, fantasies, memories, our usual ways of perceiving, and all else we can conceive as belonging to who we are. It is as if in an instant, we take a sword and cut the connections that link us to the familiar world. Cutting the connections happens so quickly and so subtly that without our careful observation, it goes unnoticed. This moment is nonetheless extremely important because the guardians come into action in a concentrated way only at the moment this severing occurs. And the severing must occur if we are to open to this realm and not filter it through what we already know.

We can easily verify this moment by simply placing our attention at the very moment of stillness. This moment is subtle but quite obvious. As soon as we come near this realm of Silence, all other connections depart. It is important that we observe this, for it tells us that all the contents of our ordinary consciousness keep us protected not only from Silence but from a direct encounter with the guardians. Our usual consciousness is a protection from spiritual presences: that is, if we yield to the noise of the world, we in turn are not attacked head on by the guardians of the threshold. If we reject the protection, the scaffolding that holds us up in the world suddenly falls away and we come to the doorway of Silence. At that moment we are as nothing, a mere void that will be immediately filled either by the guardians of Silence or, if we are prepared, by the presence of Silence. As long as our thoughts, fantasies, memories, and usual consciousness prevails, the border remains closed. When opened, however, we cannot just walk on in. We have to confront anxiety, maybe even a certain degree of terror. I am speaking here of the conscious practice of entering Silence, which differs considerably from those times when Silence comes as a gift. We want to discover the ways to take gifted moments as conscious invitations to become true servants.

We must approach Silence in the right way and with the right attitude, which is not the attitude that says look at all the good, all the virtue, all the merit, all the deepening, all the creativity, peace, sensitivity, and ability to be more present in the world that we will get out of practicing Silence. We do not enter the realm of Silence for ourselves but to honor, give attention to, care for, give homage to and acknowledge the sacredness of the realm, and to gradually come to know its terrain with a decidedly different kind of knowing. Otherwise, our interest is nothing more than ego inflation. Silence must be recognized and honored as a holy and autonomous realm. We can easily become interested in Silence for what we think it can give us. But, in the face of its true reality, we are continually humbled and made aware that we are not adequate to be with Silence when relying on our own ordinary abilities.

The esoteric tradition continually warns us that crossing a threshold without preparation brings dire results. When, for example, the threshold to the spiritual world is crossed without sufficient preparation, we can be assailed by psychosis, or an inability of our consciousness to return to ordinary reality. When the threshold of Silence is crossed without preparation, we begin to feel assailed by all kinds of images, fantasies, confusing ideas, strange associations, assaults, inner voices, and attacks; and all kinds of feelings of anger, lust, envy, and hatred. St. Anthony experienced these assaults as real beings:

> When it was nighttime they made such a crashing noise that the whole place seemed to be shaken by a quake. The demons, as if breaking through the building's four walls, and seeming to enter through them, were changed into the forms of beasts and reptiles. The place immediately was filled with the appearances of lions, bears, leopards, bulls and serpents, asps, scorpions and wolves, and each of these moved in accordance with its form ... and altogether the sounds of all the creatures that appeared were terrible, and their ragings were fierce.

A scene such as this is depicted on a panel called "The Temptations of St. Anthony," which is part of the Isenheim Altarpiece, painted in the sixteenth century by Matthias Grünewald. In the painting, a bearded old St. Anthony, dressed in a sky-blue cloak, is being dragged across the ground by several of these beasts, which look even more fierce than the description just quoted: they resemble creatures in a Bosch painting. Creatures drag him and others watch, while the whole place is filled with monstrous and, to be truthful, quite amusing beings. Some look like stupid, drooling dogs, others like winged demons. One is a large, scaly bird, another an ugly creature carrying a large club. Up in the trees and on wall ledges perch dark, winged beings waiting for the right moment to descend and pick the bones clean. Dragged through the midst of this, St. Anthony laughs uproariously. In a corner sits a more human-like small creature, with skin green and diseased, and wearing a red fool's hat. This creature is crucial: his line of vision points upward; his eye unwaveringly placed on a spot of golden light in the sky where a figure, not quite discernible, seems to be sitting.

The odd and wonderful aspect of the picture is St. Anthony's laughter, which is possible because he knows the difference between the illusion and reality of Silence. And it is possible also because of the presence of the green-skinned, pockmarked little figure in the corner wearing the fool's hat. This being is not part of the team of assailants. He is quite mysterious, though surely art historians and critics have much to say about him. I feel that he represents us all in our neglected instinctual spirit-being, and that St. Anthony's capacity to go through the assault of the guardians while never losing connection with the spiritual worlds is the work of this protecting being. The instinctual spirit is a most important figure, and it is virtually unknown in most spiritual practices. We usually look upward and outward for the spirit. The fact is, though, we could never make connection with the "higher spirit" if there were not the presence of the instinctual spirit within each of us. St. John the Baptist is such an image in relation to Christ. In iconography, St. John is always depicted wearing animal clothing, an indication that there is an instinctual yearning for the spirit, a yearning that issues from a natural instinctual spirit.

The blue cloak of St. Anthony indicates a purified soul. He is as clear as the blue of the sky itself. The purified soul makes possible complete concentration on the golden light of the spiritual world. These guardian beings have no power over him because they have no access to his soul.

The painting is a picture of Silence and of the purification needed to enter the realm of Silence. It gives us many clues that help us explore such a realm. Silence does not take us out of the noisy world; we are still dragged around by it, but we can be amused by its tactics and its crudeness. The suffering spirit-being, that small creature in the corner of the Grünewald painting wearing the fool's hat, is really the suffering of our elemental body-spirit when separated from our spirit-self. The suffering elemental body is also the suffering of the earth, as our elemental body is composed of the same elements as the earth and shares in her life. If we serve Silence, we are also serving the earth. And if we yield to the world of noise, of cacophony, then the earth suffers disease.

We cannot help but notice that St. Anthony does not fight against the creatures threatening him and dragging him around, or against those waiting to pounce for the final kill. This scene tells us that as we try to enter Silence and encounter anxiety, fear, fantasy, stupid thoughts, and buzzing impulses, we get nowhere if we try to fight them off. In the painting, St. Anthony makes no attempt to kill them. We suspect that they are somehow a necessary part of our wholeness. They may be present so that we can develop the inner strength of concentration needed to keep our focus on the spiritual worlds. When we receive the gift of

Silence by walking in the forest, for example, we form no such capacities. That walk does not help us find Silence in the noisy world; it only makes us want to get away from it. But if we begin working to find inner Silence in the midst of the loudness of the daily world, as depicted in St. Anthony's assault, we form such a capacity.

How do we know that the creatures are deceptive beings but that the presence above in the sky is not? This was an important question for St. Anthony. Once, in the desert, he saw a large silver chalice of great beauty, just sitting there. He immediately pronounced it a deception: there are no silver chalices in the desert. There was nothing around from which it could have come. There were no thieves who could have brought it from elsewhere. Like St. Anthony, when we seem to have found Silence, we must have the inner capacity to know if we are being deluded. We are deluded, for example, if we feel that we have found inner silence on our own, out of our own efforts. In the painting, the spot of golden light that holds the fool's gaze is also a moment of grace. Silence comes as grace.

And there is a very different quality to the delusion of silence than to the gift of Silence. When we are in the delusion of silence, we may notice a kind of equivalent to St. Anthony's suddenly finding a silver chalice: the quality is just too sparkly. Silence then seems to be a doubling of itself, which we experience emotionally as a tingling right down into our flesh. Silence does have a bodily aspect, but it is not this kind of excited, sparkly tingling. When such an experience happens, we are to notice it but not fight against it. A major aspect of working with Silence is learning discernment at the soul and spirit level. That is, we learn to discern different qualities of soul and spirit states by being within them while in the surround of Silence. So it is not bad nor is it a failing to encounter the delusion of silence. It is part of the learning we need.

The crucial importance of soul discernment is well illustrated by a story that Athanasius tells in his biography of St. Anthony:

> An old man, Heron, had made of fasting an inflexible and absolute law.... The angel of Satan was received by him as an angel of light, and with great honor (because he was so exhausted from fasting). Eager to obey the angel, Heron threw himself head over heels into a well, the bottom of which the eye could not perceive. In doing this, he placed his trust in the promise that had been made to him that, as a result of his meritorious works and virtues, in the future he would be proof against all danger.... Thus, as just the middle of the night arrived, he threw himself to the bottom of the well with the thought of proving his rare merit by coming out in one piece. However, the brothers had great difficulty in pulling him out half dead. He passed away two days later.

One of the ways we enter the delusion of silence is to do it all ourselves: to put all the effort of our will into trying to make the experience happen, or to think that practicing the discipline of Silence will gain us some merit. Our effort is not so much to avoid the pitfalls, however, as to develop the inner capacities of discerning very subtle differences among various qualities of Silence: to know that if we approach Silence through the emotional soul, it will produce illusory images or feelings; and to know that when we approach Silence through the spiritual-soul, it produces an inner feeling-knowing that is unlikely to be imagery but is definitely a presence of an intangible but palpable soul-substance. When we are in Silence, our body—unlike our emotions—undergoes the resonating effects of moving currents that we feel everywhere and deeply. Could it be that the fluids of the body resonate with the movements of the spiritual beings of Silence? It is not so important to know what is there (that will come in time) but to notice the body in Silence. It is important that we are able to discern the difference between this kind of feeling and an emotional reaction to the presence of Silence.

Perhaps the subtlest and the most important quality of Silence is the one given in the Grünewald painting. The guardian figure in the corner with the fool's hat keeps his eye on the golden figure in the sky. Not only does this image convey the knowledge, in a feeling way, that Silence is a spiritual act of the soul rather than a psychological state, it also tells us that Silence is always right here and infinitely far away. Both at the same time. And it tells that we are present to Silence only when our soul is deeply humbled. Along with this "feeling knowledge" comes an immediate sense of the unending vertical depth of Silence. At first, it seems that this depth, from surface to infinity, is of one uniform soul substance. However, this depth is filled with differing qualities. They occur everywhere within the depth and also seem to differ depending upon how deep we go into Silence. To explore the qualities of the depth of Silence becomes work, a very strange and difficult work.

After a while, when we get over the initial glow of entering the world of Silence, we find that exploring it does not immediately renew our energy but can be rather tiring. It takes some physical effort to remain alert within Silence and to perceive spiritually what is there. The guardians of Silence are very aware of this effort, and there comes a time when they test us to see whether we will continue or not. Such a test was well known to St. Anthony:

> Another time, as I was fasting, the Deceiver appeared to me in the figure of a hermit, who offered bread and then gave me the following advice: "Hold yourself upright, sustain your heart with bread and water, and rest a little from the multitude of your works; for you are a human being, and no matter what pretensions you may have, you are burdened with a body. Be fearful of suffering and unpleasantness." I, however, considered his sympathy and held back my words. I turned in the silence to my steadfast way and began to supplicate my Lord in prayer and said: "Lord, make him as nothing, just as

throughout all time you have been wont to make him a nothing." And when I had finished these words, he was consumed
and vanished like dust and in the manner of smoke.

It is interesting, isn't it? We feel refreshed and renewed by Silence; to
come to a point where we actually feel more tired than when we began
alarms us. I do not think that being within this realm really tires us,
though. Once we recognize that such tiredness is illusion, it diminishes.

Tiredness can also result from our sense of nearness and yet infinite
distance within Silence. That paradoxical feeling can set up an inner
effort so that we try to close the gap of the distance, which, no matter
how hard we try, does not close. The moment we catch on that there is
indeed an effort of our will going on, we can feel a tightness in our muscles, and then, with the effort of relaxing our body, the tiredness again
lessens. To remain within the terrain of Silence takes effort without effort.
Such a new capacity has to be learned. In the meditative tradition, such
a capacity is called concentration without effort. When we find such a
state, the particular region of the body that is in tension relaxes and feels
for a few moments as if it is vibrating. Tiredness that results from resting
in the Silence is also due to the new learning going on. We are learning
in a very direct way what it is like to be within an infinite realm, but as
we are doing so bodily, the infinite realm reveals itself to us in the finite.
Our body cannot initially tolerate the power of this infinite region. Too
much Silence, which is anything but inert and passive, comes in.

Trying to be in the Silence with too strong an effort indicates that
we may be working within a misunderstanding of Silence. We may have
unknowingly imagined Silence as a void, as nothing. Our effort, then,
along with the exhaustion from that effort, comes from trying to keep
not only the distracting guardians at bay but also Silence itself. And
Silence, rather than emptiness, is the living presence of a whole realm.

As we cross the border into the realm of Silence, where we meet with anxiety, fear, trepidation, seduction, and distraction, it is important that we remain alert to the tricky way these experiences move our attention away from the threshold. The purification of soul just spoken of requires inner clarity. When we do not have inner clarity, we project whatever we have not confronted within our soul onto others, and others then become the guardians of the threshold; others then seem to be keeping us from the Silence. For example, someone once drove into the driveway of our Spiritual Psychology Center and immediately said to the people in the car that she saw a large, dark being looming over the building. She did not know that she was seeing her own projection. Apparently she had some dark things to work on and instead was seeing what could be worked on in the Center. How do we know, though, that this image was something belonging to the soul of the person and not an actual confronting of a dark being? It is like asking, as we look at the Grünewald painting, "Are all those creatures merely the projection of St. Anthony's soul, or are they actual presences, guardians of the threshold of Silence?"

Projections usually do not take the form of seeing various presences in the world, except for aspiring clairvoyants. When, however, we find ourselves avoiding Silence by saying that we have to take care of others, or when others in our lives seem to be creating such emotional chaos that we cannot be quiet enough to be receptive to Silence, we are projecting. When our soul projects, it seems as if what appears is totally unconnected with ourselves. We do not realize that we are involved in what appears. When we have the capacity of inner seeing, it is possible to see, for example, a looming, dark presence because we are seeing through our soul. There is not a separation between ourselves and what we are seeing. We each become aware that what we are seeing is also what we need to be working on. That kind of inner clarity is soul purification. But purification does not mean that our soul is to be clear of presences so that the Silence can enter into a purified soul. Rather, purification means presence to our soul states. When we are aware that the guardians of Silence also reside within the soul, we have disarmed them. They diminish. We can enter into the Silence without their interference.

As we approach the Silence, the new ways of the guardians have to be taken into account. We would not expect them to function in the same ways they did in earlier times. The outward presence the of guardian beings in the Grünewald painting has become our inner psychology. However, even though the guardians work through our complexes, they are not personal. These presences are objective and real, but they now function through the medium of the psyche.

Massive maze of a building, *walking on and on in a labyrinthine direction that is not a direction except in how I keep moving forward, as in the direction my face is facing. Not lost really, but seeming to be wandering around in semidarkness. It is empty here, but I know I am not alone. Passing through room after room, the silence haunts and protects, frightens and consoles. It is not just the dark, the strangeness, the creeping cobwebs, or the threatening closed doors.... It is the confounded silence itself that can be neither invaded nor accepted. To allow it to remain, I am its persecuted slave; to break it open with sound, I become the known and located interloper— discovered, found out, subject to all the hidden demons it could then unleash. Can I face them? Defeat them? Hide in a place safe enough to be protected?*

There are no answers in the silence ... listening ... straining every fiber of ear and eye, smell and taste...the silence brushing against me and weighing into my chest so that I can barely breathe. At the moment of losing consciousness, the silence penetrates my skin and enters the wholeness of my body ... oh!

Ahhhhhh ... so that's it! Of course there is no answer in the silence ... the answer is the silence. At this moment of meeting, I awake and forget.

— Cheryl Sanders-Sardello

CHAPTER 3

Entering the Silence

We can find the realm of Silence. We can learn practices for entering this realm and for experiencing the many interpenetrating currents of its landscape. The practice of entering into the Silence is neither exclusively a soul work nor exclusively a spiritual work: it is a work of the embodied spiritual-soul, the whole person. We are not helped very much by working with well-known soul practices such as active imagination, images, and dreams. Nor are we helped very much by working with spiritual practices, such as concentration, meditation, or contemplation, in traditional ways. Both soul and spirit practices do involve and assume the presence of Silence, but both focus on what occurs within the Silence rather than on the medium itself. A further factor enters: Silence is experienced bodily. We sense the presence of Silence and, after being with Silence over a period of time, we find distinct changes in our body that contribute to our capacity to enter and stay within the Silence. Thus the practice of entering Silence itself forms the instrument that gives us access to the Silence.

If we do not enter the Silence through sensing, we are sure to approach it as personal solitude, or as a reality of soul within, or as a private spiritual experience having nothing to do with the world. Entering Silence through sensing is the key to living both our soul life and our spiritual life in the world. It responds to those who say, "Change yourself first, and then go out and change the world." This standard way of trying to bring soul and spirit into conjunction with the world does not work. Letting Silence pervade all we do does work because it never separates itself from the world. Thus we do not make the practice of Silence exclusively into a soul work and go inward, nor exclusively a spiritual work to attain some goal on a spiritual path. The work is to be with Silence itself, and in so doing we are one with soul, spirit, body, and world. When practiced over time, we find it becomes possible to be with Silence in all that we do, and in our doing, our presence in the world works as a healing force.

The remarkable writer Frank Waters speaks of the presence of Silence in the world in his description of the Pueblo Indian Way:

> They sat faces bowed, eyes downward, wrapped in blankets, swathed in Silence. But this silence was pregnant with the ever-living mystery; and the tentacles of mind and heart groped through it to feel its shape and form and substance… When the guttural Indian voice finally stops there is silence. A silence so heavy and profound that it squashes the kernel of truth out of his words, and leaves the meaningless husks mercilessly exposed … and the silence grows round the walls, hands from one to another, until all the silence is one silence, and that silence is the meaning of all.

Silence here is directly sensed, a palpable mystery, an essence that is also a form. Notice the beautiful language. He says they were "swathed in Silence," bound, wrapped, protected, covered, lovingly held. Such Silence pervades the space and makes us keenly aware of our defects and insufficiencies. Rumi similarly understands what Silence does when he says, "Now I'll be quiet and let silence separate what is true from what are lies as thrashing does." And Kabir, too:

> Be silent in your mind, silent in your senses,
>> and also silent in your body.
> Then, when all these are silent, don't do anything.
>> In that state truth will reveal itself to you.
> It will appear in front of you and ask,
>> "What do you want?"

A commitment to silence is a commitment to truth. This truth is found first in the truth of sensing. Not forgetful sensing, but being present in our sensing. When we do so, our sight is clearer, our smelling keener, our touching more intimate. This experience is not one of a stronger acuity of the senses but rather of a sensing pervaded with the holiness of the world. Commitment is the best place to start with Silence. It is then possible to move to the depths and the heights, but if we try to go to these regions first, we are assured only of illusion.

We need not do anything to increase the sensitivity of our sensing other than to be present to what happens when we experience Silence in the midst of the natural world. We said that Silence gathers in nature. Instead of simply enjoying nature's silence, however, our initial practice consists of noticing what happens when we are within the Silence, for we are within a very active presence.

We feel the presence of Silence throughout the physical world as a kind of touch, like that of a warm breeze on the skin on a fall day. We feel its presence as a living surround that fills us within. Our whole body, as sensory organ in itself, senses this realm. We cannot say we experience Silence just in front of us, or to one side, or above, or in back of us. It is all around and also within, and yet it has the quality of a complete Other. This intimate Other actively produces our soul experience of being an individual of embodied spirit in the world. This bodily experience cures us of the disease of dualism, for in feeling the depth of the spirit-body's individuality we leave the illusion of a self that is located somewhere inside us and enter into the fullness of the reality of being a whole person. Being a whole person means we experience what it is like to be body, soul, and spirit as one. Soul practices take us out of this wholeness and into thinking, feeling, willing, and imaginal consciousness; spiritual practices result in out-of-body experiences and remove us from our wholeness. It is Silence that gives our living body its solitude, its oneness with soul and spirit. We experience it in a somatic way, as an aloneness that partakes of the whole of the world. We feel isolated within our individual ego, but if we move out of it just a little bit and begin sensing our own bodily presence, we feel the touch of Silence announce itself, and we have found the way out of self-absorption.

Sensing our body presence does not mean knowing about it, looking at it from a spectator perspective, or just feeling it from within. It means we can actually feel our bodily presence in its wholeness as if touched from the outside. To feel so requires us to shift our attention out of our thoughts and perceptions of what is around us to the familiarity and closeness of our own bodily form. For a few moments, as we shift, we do not shut out the world but rather feel it as a spiritual presence touching us. In those few moments we feel subtly touched all over.

The most basic experience of Silence is intimacy. We feel an intimacy with the world, as if we are within everything around us rather than behind or alongside things that we are then looking at. This mantle of touch brings us to the living truth of our being. We know who we are in a completely non-self-conscious way. We feel how we, in our individuality, are part of a vast and mysterious world process. And when we cultivate Silence to the point that we are consciously within it rather than imagining that it is in us, we cannot be other than we are. The imagination of it being within us emanates from the loss of the touch of Silence, for without sensing this intimate touch we too easily think we are whatever we want to be or others want us to be. Silence keeps us intimately bound with the truth of our being, constantly conveying to us in a bodily way that our individual and unique presence as soul, spirit, and body intermingles with the world and, at the same time, lives a free and independent existence.

Illusion and ego-fantasy begin with forgetting this intimacy. When our forgetfulness of the touch of Silence becomes severe, we experience anxiety. The currents of intimate touch are then overcome by another kind of touch that makes our skin crawl, gives us goose bumps, and raises the hair on our arms and back of our neck. This is an anti-silence, which we get used to in the world of noise. Anti-silence makes us into immobile and frozen automatons, at the mercy of those in charge of collective, mass consciousness. Or, it makes us automatons of the past, going around in the world repeating what we are told we need to be by others. Our anxiety comes from our bodily experience of being reduced to the likeness of everyone else, of being completely forgetful of the touch that gives us a unique sensing of our bodily presence in the world. All the adornments, make-up, clothing, and accoutrements can never individualize the way we sense the fullness of our embodied being.

Silence is a work as well as a phenomenon. If we step into this form of intimacy to feel its touch through conscious effort rather than happy circumstance, we open up, if we wish, a continual work. For the touch of Silence does not stay with us. There is too much within us that overpowers that initial touch. How can we stay in touch with Silence when our soul is filled with noises of every sort: the incessant inner talking that goes on; the continual churning of our emotions; angers that have gone unresolved for years; envies, hatreds, desires, bad memories, pains and hurts, deceits we have justified to ourselves? And even more than that, when a sleepiness of soul makes us value our comfort above all else and ensures that we do not have to confront all this noise.

When we are touched by the ineffable in the way of intimacy, we begin to face all the inner noise, for we have aroused the guardians of Silence. All of this noise, and much more, gradually has to be burned away. Noise that goes on way beneath the surface probably from life-times—noise that we have no inkling is there—begins to come up and float around like debris of a shipwreck. But as we begin to sense this debris, we are held safely within the surround of Silence. There is no need for us to sink down into all that noise and resolve it therapeutically before entering the world of quiet, for Silence is in itself therapeutic. We discover bits of the noise gradually, and Silence reveals how to clear them. Typically we are shown our inner noise by something in the world. We may find ourselves around continual busyness, rudeness, and callous-ness. We may perceive noisiness coming back to us from what we had projected previously onto other people, which now as it comes to meet us, we know it comes from out of ourselves. We are perceptually faced with some version of our inner noise and are usually shocked in a way that amuses us.

The way of Silence is more joyful than most other spiritual work mainly because it is not a path at all, and only requires that we look around and "feel." And as we notice these qualities of noise, it is possi-ble to clear them, though not by doing anything in particular. Each time we notice some new noise we also find it possible to go even deeper into the Silence, and it is this deepening that does the clearing.

After we have sufficiently contemplated the Silence that we meet in the natural world, and we have found the way into sensing a new body, we can begin to enter Silence through meditation, but not until then, or it will revert to a standard spiritual practice, and we will bypass the depths of Silence in order to get to one or another spiritual goal. Get-ting started is deceptively easy. Each day at an appointed time, go to a quiet place, a room where you will not be disturbed. Sit in a comfort-able chair, both feet firmly on the floor, body perfectly relaxed, and as near as possible do not think of anything. This may be hard to do the first two or three times. Relaxation of the body is crucial. The desire body is reflected in the muscles of the body, so when body tension exists you will find that you cannot be receptive to the Silence.

An important detail concerns rhythm. This practice is to be done in the same place, at the same appointed time each day, and if possible, for the same length of time each day. Doing the practice daily for fifteen or twenty minutes is adequate. After several weeks the time can be lengthened and a new rhythm started. Rhythm is as important as the practice itself because it brings us into harmony with the great rhythms governing the world: the rhythms of the growth and death of plants, the rhythms of the movement of the planets and the stars, the rhythms of the tides under the influence of the moon, and the rhythms of all organisms. It also joins us in harmony to the rhythms of the organs of our own body: to our heartbeat, breath, digestion, and pulse of the blood, and to all of the organs. These rhythms, in turn, reflect the movements of the planets. Through taking up a meditation practice rhythmically, we join ourselves to the larger world and to the cosmos. Silence belongs to these great undulations, maybe even as their keeper and protector.

The semi-upright position is important, as is having our feet on the ground, for it is the body's expression of the individuality of our I-being. In practicing Silence we are not trying to merge with the cosmos or to leave this world for timeless regions but to imagine Silence as radiating everywhere, expanding in all directions. The image of expansion goes together with the incarnational spirituality being suggested here. This posture ensures that we are sufficiently in our body, that we do not leave the world, but are relaxed enough that we can enter into a mode of consciousness different from waking consciousness. We are not pulled toward trance, though. The position is one of alertness.

Engaging in this practice for a while, usually a long while, maybe several years, results in an intensified body-sensibility. We start to sense the presence, at the edges of our body, of extremely subtle currents that have a unique quality. These currents are neither "energy" nor the electromagnetic currents of the body. Such terms are borrowed from physics and carry with them no sense of an actual living presence, only objective and materialistic forces. We experience the currents of Silence, however, as being touched by a spiritual presence. The description here is accurate because it is not like being touched by a body, or like being inside ourselves, but like being within an active, interior world that has been waiting for us. The whole nature of the currents of Silence is that of the presence of an interiority. It is like knowing someone in the most intimate way, as if that someone has poured his or her heart out to us, not in a sentimental way, but in a way that reveals the very essence of that being.

I am speaking not only of extremely subtle experiences but also of experiences that cannot be understood literally. The descriptions here are imaginal descriptions; that is, they are expressions of an imaginative, yet very real, presence to the phenomena. It is necessary to hear such descriptions with an "as if" kind of constant living quality. In fact, the presence of Silence teaches this kind of consciousness. When we initially experience Silence, it seems that we can find no words to say what the experience consists of. Gradually, the vast interiority begins to differentiate itself "as if" spirit beings are present, and we can discern different qualities among them. We are not in a void or in a static state but in an active presence of differentiated presences. The word *currents* is the best and most accurate term we can find to describe it.

We can develop the description even further. When we feel touched by the presence of an active, living interiority, it is necessary for us to notice that there is only one way that this is possible: it is an interiority turned inside out. When someone speaks to us or touches us, we have the sense that there, within that person facing us, is an interiority. Silence does not touch us in this way. Instead, we experience an immediacy of the quality of interiority. There is nothing behind Silence or within it. It is a total "within." And whatever is within it is not within it in the way objects are in a container; whatever occurs within Silence becomes one of the currents of Silence. When we are in the Silence we experience something very bodily, and we also experience it as a subtle touch at the level of our soul, at the level of our own interiority.

To be fully with Silence requires that we develop a capacity to be present to both the most subtle qualities of objective touch imaginable and to the manner in which this touch resonates the soul interiorly. That is, to be fully present to this experience, we have to be inside ourselves and outside ourselves at the same time. It is also possible in practice to alternate between emphasizing the interior quality by putting our attention at the level of the interior of the body and then emphasizing the exterior quality by putting our attention at the level of the outer form of our body. Alternating attention like this while we are in Silence can help us come to experience the fullness of the phenomenon. This practice, however, needs to be accompanied by one through which we experience the border between the interior and exterior, between the objective touch and the resonance of it.

One of the basic qualities of these currents is a pulsating motion— a motion, not something that is in motion, for silence is not spatial. That is why when we sense it, it is not before us or in back of us or at any spatial location. And yet, it is "as if" spatial. We feel the quality of touch as if someone were subtly touching us all over, not just at one point on our body. This sense of touch has more of the quality of a process in time rather than an event that happens and then rests quietly. Such a quality gives our sense of touch a different sensibility from that of being touched by someone. It is not exactly like being stroked either, because the pulsating movement is more like a friendly phantom, or even an angel, contacting and moving through us.

A second basic quality of the currents of Silence as interiority-felt-exteriorly is the quality of whirling. The motion of the currents does not seem to be linear in any fashion. While saying that the motion has the form of something like vortices seems too precise; it is something belonging to that order of motion, although we have to imagine multiple interpenetrating vortices. Again, we do not see this form but feel it.

The third quality of the currents of Silence is that when they touch us, it is as if they slow down and start to fold within themselves. We then experience depth as layers of Silence. When practiced, we can move our attention into their various folds. These folds are not visual but an imaginal expression. This description, as well as the two previous ones, are meant to convey a feeling-quality. The descriptions can be helpful only if they are not taken literally. It is important that we not look for these qualities of pulsing, whirling, and layering but simply notice gradually that Silence has complex characteristics. Getting to know these characteristics is getting to know the presences, the spirit-beings, the currents of Silence.

The layered quality just described leads us into even more complex subtlety. When we are within Silence, we experience the quality of layering in two different ways. We feel as if we are within something analogous to an etheric, viscous medium that sometimes quite suddenly alters in its viscosity. Such alteration produces the sense we have of going through different layers of a medium. The second way we experience the quality of layering has to do with the different depths within Silence. We sense these depths, even while they interpenetrate each other, as something akin to different layers.

The currents of Silence that have just been described center on the quality of rhythm. Because rhythm predominates—with all of the other qualities being modifications and contributors to it, the region of the body where Silence enters to spread instantly throughout the whole of our body is the heart. The qualities described are much harder to feel when we, in Silence, are focused in the region of the head. They can be felt there, to be sure, but the subtlety of the forces is much greater in the heart region. The qualities described are also difficult to feel in the lower regions of the body. If attention goes there when we are entering Silence, the qualities of movement tend to merge into a single strong feeling of Silence without nuances.

Because we are taken into the soul-spirit nature of the world through Silence, when the kind of meditative practice described is carried out, our bodily presence in the world is immediately influenced. This characteristic differentiates the practice from any other kind of inner meditative work. Within other forms of meditation, we may experience change within ourselves, but only gradually, if we are fortunate, do these inner changes spread out into the world. We change unmistakably in our bodily presence when we have worked even slightly with the currents described. It is important, however, not to go looking for these various currents. To do so would introduce too strong a mental component into the meditative practice. The currents are always present, and gradually, as we practice, the kinds of differences described here become evident, if we have enough presence of mind to notice them.

The varied qualities of Silence have been enumerated so that we may gradually come to experience the complex nature of Silence and in experiencing its complexity begin to feel something quite extraordinary. We begin to have moments in which we experience ourselves as Time Beings, not beings in time. This is the remarkable result of our spending time in Silence. And as we more fully experience what it is like to be a Time Being, Silence more and more characterizes our countenance.

What is it to experience being a Time Being? Silence is completely active in the most quiet way imaginable. When we are within it, we become a fullness of activity. We usually think being active means our body is doing something of an exterior nature: it walks, runs, and jumps about from one activity to another. We are then something that also acts. When we are within this realm of Silence, our sense of activity is radically different. There is no longer an entity that does things; there is only the doing within of which we are conscious. This activity has the quality of duration, an interior time experience that is not measured by the clock. Within the moving currents of duration, we feel that space has collapsed into the time experience. The currents, while being all movement in duration, feel spatial. Our mind cannot comprehend such a quality, but if we attend to our sensing within the Silence we can feel these paradoxical qualities.

The danger of describing phenomena in such a way as this is that what is meant as help instead becomes a hindrance. It would be possible to speak of Silence in an evocative way that makes the soul resonate with the experience, but that would draw us to the phenomenon without helping us enter into it. It would give us an illusive spectator perspective that would evoke our emotions and excite an experience, but it would not help us develop the capacities to explore the phenomenon. These descriptions are meant to further the practices that get us to the threshold of Silence, past the guardians of the threshold, and into the interiority of Silence, and there to sense its subtle, transformative activity. Further, these kinds of descriptions are necessary as a way to verify that Silence is a true phenomenon that consists of far more than stillness and quiet. Carefulness is needed to ensure that we are not spuriously attributing characteristics to what we may be experiencing.

LYING IN THIS PLACE, *under heaven, the weight of the light coming from the stars pins me to the earth as surely as a butterfly is pinned to a display box.*

Lying here in this place, on this spot, affixed yet floating, I submit to the law of silence that seals the earth as loveletter and sends it hurtling through space on its mysterious mission.

Lying on the earth, glued to its grassy skin by the sweat of my own body, I obey the weight of silence pressing me closer to the envelope.

Lying in the silence of necessity, I complete the emblematic. Separation is the myth, isolation the unreal. A distinct and utter YES is spoken by this silence that resonates in and around all that I am, permeating everything from atoms to organs, from Adam to resurrection.

Lying silently, Silence silences my incessant questions and bathes them in the soothing stream of silence.

I am cleansed.

— *Cheryl Sanders-Sardello*

CHAPTER 4

Relating within Silence

We are imagining Silence within the natural world as a near ideal instance of the experience we seek, and we are learning to explore the ways of this phenomenon by engaging in a singular kind of meditative attention. In attending to our relationships, we can also learn of the ways that Silence enters, and we can cultivate its presence. It then proves to have a marvelous nurturing and spiritual power. I have seen personal relationships, which, lived in usual ways, simply could not last, transform into entirely new forms of relating in the world. Relationships, then, give us an additional way to access and get to know the ways of this vast interiority of Silence.

In close relationships we get into difficulty with each other through either speaking or not speaking. We say something that hurts the other person, or we hold in our feelings and do not speak, and then pressure builds to the point of anger. This overly simplified observation suggests that we can attend Silence in our relating through our speaking. We can discover through the way we speak with one another how Silence can shape and form what goes on between us into something holy and sacred, even in the most mundane moments. Obviously, we are focusing on something other than the deadly form of silence that often intrudes and takes over relationships once wounding has taken place. That kind of silence, with its toxic character, comes from egoistic withholding of holy Silence from the interior space of relating. In such instances, silence itself becomes the poison rather than the fecund, creating element. How we speak and don't speak can either keep Silence away or invite it to be the central aspect of relating.

Speaking that takes the form of narration, which tells *about* experience rather than speaking from within it, does not allow for a vivid presence of Silence. Human speech, fortunately, does not naturally follow the pattern of narration, though we show strong elements of that pattern when we speak with no listening around our speaking. We are in that pattern of narration when we wait impatiently, with nervous pauses, for the other person to finish a sentence so we can talk about what we want to talk about. This narrating form of language, which derives from the dominance of the printed word, makes us godlike ego spectators to our own experience, and thus spectators and controllers of others and of the wider world. Such a pattern of speaking, running one word right into the other without pause, covers over the realm of Silence.

The pauses in speech are places where Silence can enter to change completely the character, sense, meaning, and feeling of what we say. The strongest element of inner noise consists of endless narratives speaking in our heads. This inner narrator even governs the manner in which we are present to images and feelings. It is as if we have an inner tour guide to the galleries and museums of the mind, constantly separating ourselves from ourselves. This narrator then becomes externalized in our speaking, and as it does so, we are no longer fully present within our speaking. It is as if speaking begins to pour out of us like words on a computer screen. Under such conditions, there is no space for Silence.

A first entry into the Silence between ourselves and others is to appreciate the pause, the stumbling, the inarticulateness, the gaps, and the searching that accompany speaking. These "holes" in our speaking are not themselves the bearers of Silence, but they are foyers within which we are able to listen for the approach of Silence, for the beckoning of the ineffable. Listening is required for the soul of speech to live, a listening that does not come only before and after we speak but within our speaking itself. This special kind of listening waits patiently, without the need to fill in any emptiness. We can easily feel when we are speaking in this manner rather than conveying information or letting the chatter in our mind spill out endlessly.

Relating of any sort always contains an element of power and the need to feel in charge. When we open up to another, even in the most minimal way, we risk losing ourselves. We subconsciously know this and become extremely anxious when there are gaps in our conversation. When communication concerns only two individuals, there is really no way around this situation of power, but the intimate conversation of love changes this somewhat, so it is a good way to imagine what speaking in the Silence is like. Ordinary conversation forgets this intimacy. Thus there are two factors to overcome if we are to allow Silence into our speaking: the tendency for the structure of the written word, or narration, to replace the original qualities of speech; and the subconscious need for power over the other person, which uses this tool of automatic, rapid speech.

A sense of rhythm plays the central role in our finding a new way of relating through our speaking. When we say one or a few words and then pause, a rhythm is set up. This rhythm cannot be affected, however, for it comes forth from the phrasal structure of the language itself rather than from the words we use to maintain a feeling of control. Words themselves, when spoken from within rather than narrated, contain an inherent rhythm and self-instruct us to pause in just the right way. Two elements are needed to establish rhythm: the words themselves and the pauses. When pauses ease into and over the words, the character of the words change. They become filled with soul because a word that is open

49

to Silence resonates with our own soul being, which in turn resonates with the words and spreads even into the pauses. It is as if we are building a house for Silence, which can then come in and powerfully alter what goes on in the relationship.

We can experientially verify this process in an easy way. For example, we can repeat a short sentence in varying ways to let the pauses enter into the sentence:

I   enter   the   silence.

I enter   the   silence.

I   enter   the silence.

We can feel how Silence builds its presence through the rhythm, while changing the quality of the sentence. The sentence is now something very different from saying, "I enter the silence." The need for rush cools. The skill, of course, is in our letting rhythm in without affectation and without making it mechanical. If we practice this little meditative exercise—varying the pauses in a sentence—for five minutes daily over several months, we begin to feel the sense of rhythm within our body. We even begin to feel a need for such rhythm. We begin to anticipate Silence as the most important aspect of our conversation with others. We find ourselves inclining toward this element as the way, the only way, to be in connection with the soul of the other person. We come to feel such a connection as far more important than our curiosity, intellectual ability, need for affirmation, or anything else we might bring to what seems like a simple conversation.

Entering Silence through the manner of our participatory speaking has a different quality from entering Silence through experiencing it in the world or through meditating. It is as if, through speaking with others, we enter an entirely different realm of Silence, with its own forms related to other Silence forms, yet completely unique. Imagine two intersecting circles representing two individuals, both of whom have found the way into Silence. The place where the two circles overlap in the middle creates a special form called the *vesica*, an oblong shape. In Christian iconography. many images of Christ, Mary, and the saints have this form behind them, painted in gold. We see it in all paintings of Our Lady of Guadalupe. The form depicts the golden aura of the holy person. The *vesica*, which is multidimensional and not flat as depicted in paintings, also depicts the way Silence surrounds us. When two people are within this aura of living spirit, they can feel the holiness of the relationship. It is as if the relating is held within a holy vessel. We can think of it as the holy vessel of the heart, as if through our heart, in its relation with the heart of the beloved, we enter into a larger heart. The meeting of our heart centers creates a space for a holy third, and all three together form the center of a larger, more encompassing heart center.

When we are within the presence of living Silence, which is being created every moment by the way we speak with someone, we feel an extraordinary fullness that makes it possible to be within the soul of another without harming the other person with our needs, desires, wants, and fantasies. It is a key to a holy relationship. We feel a soul relationship so deeply, in a bodily way, that it is as if the love that exists in speaking has a shaping power, as if the Silence of the universe is, for a little while, condensed and comes to rest right where we two people are together. We experience it as an inner bodily joy and absence of strain, and we feel an immediate presence, a flow of subtle currents between our self and the other person.

Some people, quite naturally but not without effort, come to live together within the aura of Silence nearly all the time. It is not solely a function of attending to the way we speak with each other, for paying attention is merely the best entry point into this form of relating. What we learn through attending to our speaking is that relating is never a matter of only two individuals: a third presence is entailed. Relationship is as much about the presence of this third as it is about two people relating. As we attend to our speaking, we gradually begin to feel that our relationship concerns the care of this presence. We do not need to know who this presence is, but we do need to recognize that it does have much more of the quality of a "who" than simply some force or faceless form of energy.

Depth psychology has recognized something like the presence of a third in the context of psychotherapy. It is called *transference*, or, more recently, the *interactive field*. Change in therapy is not possible without entering and experiencing this field. We can consider depth psychology as the forerunner in bringing to consciousness the element of "the third." However, it never recognizes the third as the presence of Silence; instead it imagines it as a field created either by the presence of an archetypal figure or by the erotic connection between patient and therapist that substitutes for the presence of someone from the past, such as a father figure. This third of psychotherapy, when recognized, itself becomes the object of the analysis. We feel the third that is the presence of Silence in relationship as a holy presence. It transcends anything in the nature of something from our past, and it is more ineffable than an archetypal god or goddess.

People who discover that relating concerns the care of the presence of the living being of Silence enter into the spiritual path of relationship. All relationships are not of this character. I think that two individuals have to be called to this way, just as taking up any spiritual work requires the presence of grace that invites us into it. So this description of the presence of Silence in relating is not intended to say that this is the way that relating ought to happen. However, if there is not this presence between people some of the time, the relationship will be troubled. To actively cultivate this presence in a conscious way is a very special way of relating. We can know if we are called to this with our partner by simply paying attention to this third presence. If we find ourselves more and more drawn to these moments of Silence and find that the Silence itself draws us both more and more, then it is likely that our relationship is also access to Silence.

Silence is at the heart of relating. Some indications that this is so include our experiencing relationship in an inner way that is dynamic, mobile, developing, conflicting, flowing—almost anything other than static and comfortable. We find ourselves becoming intensely interested in the question of why this relationship exists. What is its spiritual source? What is its purpose, its destiny? Why are we together? These kinds of questions do not have intellectual answers. By concentrating our entire mind, body, and spirit on the space of Silence in relating, these questions come forth and so does a response. The response occurs at first by feeling ourselves disintegrating. We feel that something is going on in the relationship, and even though it may be intimate and full of love, it tears apart who we thought we were, then puts us together in a new form. We are not doing this; the forming force of Silence that we have chosen to be within instigates and guides this process.

We have all had these experiences of relating. If we are not present to the Silence, such moments feel destructive. It might be helpful for us to remember an intense encounter with someone, wherein we felt the force of something present that went beyond each of us; something numinous and beyond any inner feeling; something completely independent of us, though completely pervading us. And if it was something that we felt tearing at the relationship, we might try to remember that there was also a "friendliness" to this tearing apart, unlike the usual kind of personal destructiveness that occurs between people. As we stay with this remembrance, we come to know inwardly that whatever was going on, we had to let it go on, that whatever this was, it was in charge of the relationship. And as we stay with this remembered happening, our relating becomes stronger but more quiet, more filled with Silence. Now, we are content to look at our partner and see inner beauty, which we did not see before because we saw only what we wanted to see. Now, when we do see the beauty, we also see that it radiates into the world, adding spiritual strength to the world. Silence has allowed us to see what otherwise cannot be seen.

The presence of the other person, perceived within the aura of Silence, links us to the world in new ways. Our perception of the environs changes; the world becomes more vivid, clearer, almost transparent. The quality of the space between our self and the other person becomes tangible; it is almost as if the space is a substance that can be touched. This substantial space changes from moment to moment: it expands and contracts, becomes thinner and thicker, more opaque and then more transparent. If we attend to this kind of perception, it becomes a guide in relating to the soul and spirit being of our partner. Just noticing these qualities becomes the work of relating.

The space of relating in Silence also has a particular feeling quality. It is sacred space. We sense a calm and pervading quiet; we sense the surroundings as an inner sanctum, a sanctuary; and we both feel that we are together to honor and cultivate this sanctuary. This feeling quality is present even when there is conflict or anger. It feels as if we exist together in a dream, but it is not dreamy. In fact, we are more alert and awake than usual. But the hard edges that usually separate one thing from another are softened due to the Silence.

While not every couple is called to serve Silence in relating, such serving does seem to be the long-term intention of relating. We see it all the time. As people age in their relationship, Silence has more and more a part to play, clearly having something essential to do with relating. If

Silence does not become a conscious practice within our relationship, it shows up as a pathology of relating. Silence becomes stronger, but the capacity for it has not been developed. What then exists between a couple is cold, without soul. They live a mere existence in the same space. Each feels ignored, neglected, alone, and filled with longing. The longing does not come from the disappointment and disillusion of the couple, but from the Silence itself. It is not possible to be together, intimately close to one another, except through the cultivation of the holiness of Silence. When it has no place in our relating, we feel a heavy presence looming darkly.

Silence protects us from the illusions of relating. The primary illusion is romanticism, the hope that there is only you and I and nothing else in the world. Another illusion is thinking it possible to know the soul being of the other directly. This illusion gradually usurps the freedom of the other by not allowing his or her mystery. It results in suffocation. Another illusion is thinking that we can relate without the presence of power. Power is always an aspect of any relationship. It keeps us away from necessary vulnerability and gives the feeling of being in charge. We have to go through these illusions, but they become destructive if we are not able to find and honor the presence of the third, the Silence.

This deep mystery of relating is very different from the psychology of two people involved in relationship, such as what each brings to the relationship, the personal psychology of each, or the psychology of men and women in general. Psychology is interested in relationship in terms of how we can relate better, how we can understand the other person better, and how we can get along better in order to have a "successful" relationship. As it has developed, the psychology of relating wards off the possibility that relating is something that we do in order to find the way into Silence. It does not recognize that Silence is by nature relational. In exploring the mystery of relating, we are not shifting away from personal relationship; we are not saying that, after all, relating is really not about each other. Instead, we recognize that there is no such thing as "each other," a couple alone. Perhaps relating doesn't have so much to do with recognizing and integrating our Anima, if we are a man, and the Animus, if we are a woman, as it does inviting in holy solitude.

ENTERING YOUR ROOM *I know I am not alone with you. A holy silence attends you, too, close to your head just there by the window. It seems to have a proprietary attitude, as if you belong more to silence than to me. Your eyes quiver open for a moment then close again, but there is a hint of a smile on your pain-wracked face, and your hand moves a centimeter toward me. Sitting, holding your hand, watching you struggle between planes of existence in this room full of silence, I know you are getting to know this other presence. As a baby turns in the womb, preparing for the long journey into sound, your heart is turning in your soul, preparing for the long journey into silence. And all I can do is hold your hand and smile when your eyes flicker open for a moment and try to fill the silence with all my love, so you will know it is there, too, on your arrival into silence.*

— *Cheryl Sanders-Sardello*

CHAPTER 5

The Healing Power of Silence

S ilence heals. It does so differently than other kinds of healing. This healing does not involve manipulation of subtle energies. It also does not involve the electromagnetic currents of the body, and while the chakras may be involved, they are not the focus. The healing of Silence does not carry a medical intent; that is, its function does not center on the rapid removal of symptoms. To understand this modality of healing, we have to turn away from our modern understanding that healing functions as a medicine, and that it cannot occur without the intervention of someone trained in one or another tradition of healing. Silence is self-healing. It is a process in which a direct and nonmediated connection is made between the forces and inner currents that join the invisible worlds of Silence and the tangibility of our bodily presence and being.

We do not use Silence to heal as if it were an energy or an instrument used to bring about certain effects. We do not first go into Silence and then find another kind of force operating within the Silence that can be such an instrument. Instead, the healing currents of Silence are intrinsic to Silence itself, integral to its very nature. And healing is not just one of the results we can hope to expect when we develop the discipline of entering the Silence. It is not a result at all: as one of the inherent spiritual-soul currents within Silence, it is always present. It is possible to learn to focus on the nature and character of these healing currents, just as it is to recognize the guardians of Silence, to sense-feel the rhythms of the currents of Silence, to develop practices that enhance such experiences, and to relate to one another within Silence as a service to the world. These are all subtle qualities of silence that we can learn to detect and, when in Silence, to work with more fully and consciously.

Once we have become accustomed and comfortable being in the Silence for an extended period of time, we can begin to move consciousness around in different ways without either the Silence or ourselves within it being disturbed. We can direct consciousness because the capacity of attention is our spirit-being capacity. That is, when we have entered into the Silence, our ordinary ego-consciousness recedes into the background, and a different kind of consciousness comes forward, one best called attention. Ego is still present, for we do not go into any sort of trance state entering the Silence. However, if ego-consciousness does not recede into the background, then Silence is filled with inner chatter, thinking, fantasies, and distractions. We may have to keep returning from the excursions of ego-consciousness to the Silence itself, remembering, though, that Silence is not emptiness but an alert unfocusing focus on subtle rhythms that join our interiority to the natural world.

From time to time, we may notice that there is another presence within the Silence, our companion-presence that is a "you that is not you." It has a certain autonomy to it in a way that ego-consciousness does not have. We notice this presence out of the corner of our consciousness, so to speak. It is its own center, but we experience this center as a higher or more refined sense of ourselves. In the esoteric tradition, this presence is called the witness. This term is quite descriptive, for ego-consciousness does not know how to witness; it has to feel itself at the center of our consciousness and in charge, to the point that it identifies itself as the whole of consciousness. We first experience witness-consciousness as a kind of encompassing consciousness that we do not fully identify with, but at the moment we feel its presence, our ego-consciousness quickly reduces. It becomes a minor player in the whole of what constitutes the range of consciousness, for consciousness ranges in activity rather than functioning as a whole, uniform field. If we are to locate the presence of the healing action of Silence, we need to become acquainted with this range of activity, which goes from our usual ego-consciousness that is wholly a spectator with no sense of an interior to an awareness that we feel has no pointed focus. Our witness-consciousness observes within this range but not as some kind of observer outside of consciousness itself. Witness-consciousness, which is our own attention in the Silence, both observes and participates at the same time.

We notice witness-consciousness when, within the field of Silence, we experience the feeling of another almost adjoining field in the region right behind our head and extending downward. It has a quality of roundness and spaciousness, more like a region than a point of focus. Within this region we feel, experience, and know that whatever we engage comes out of an interior point of view; it comes spiritually. It is a non-brain-bound consciousness. It helps us learn to experience witness-consciousness independent of ordinary consciousness in relation to healing. We need just sit quietly, go into the Silence, and notice that as we do so, we seem to "slide" into a different mode of consciousness. When we relax in this way, we think we are in our usual consciousness and have simply settled in, but there is an actual shift. We can notice that the consciousness we are within, while we are in Silence, participates in the Silence. It is as if our consciousness were part of the Silence itself, while also able to observe without detachment.

With this initial act of noticing witness-consciousness, or attention, in Silence, we are in the middle of quite subtle activities. Our challenge now is to be within them without shifting into mental activity, such as trying to know exactly which activity we are within. We know we have shifted into mental activity when our experience within Silence begins to compartmentalize, and we inwardly feel as if we are in a separated state of consciousness that excludes other states. Silence, consciousness, and attention all flow into one another, but it is not difficult to focus within one or another aspect without them compartmentalizing. Within Silence, in its aspect of attention, we can also track some of the specific actions of Silence itself. For example, when we enter into the Silence and let our attention center on the interior of the body, we can feel the flow of Silence fill out the inner form of our body. As it does so, we become present to what can be described and termed the *invisible body of Silence.* This presence is the experience of our inner body, as a whole, pervaded with Silence. This body also feels as if it is transparent. That is, we do not experience our body as flesh and blood and organs. If we do, it is then our detached ego using our known physical concepts of the body and our familiar feelings and perceptions to "help" us know where we are.

It is also possible to shift our attention in Silence to the outer form of our body. When we do this, we do not feel Silence "cling" to the outer form; instead, we feel Silence extend outward without boundary. We are not carried off into an out-of-body experience, however, because Silence quietly and intimately touches the body. It helps if we shift attention from the interior, invisible body of Silence to the exterior, invisible, infinite presence of Silence touching the body, and then move our attention back and forth between the two, being present to both at the same time. We do this movement with the gentlest of will. Being present to both at the same time slightly relaxes the tension of our will as we use it to move from interior to exterior Silence.

This simple exercise of moving the attention of Silence can be practiced for a long time. It is a practice that in itself has no aim other than to acquaint us with the marvelous, indeed miraculous, flexibility of Silence. We begin to experience the wonder of Silence and find that it is far from a vague, enjoyable kind of static state that makes us feel good. We enter a whole and complete realm of Silence that invites us to explore its terrain. And the primary instrument that makes this exploration possible is our attention.

When we are able to hold the inner, invisible body of Silence together with the outer form of Silence that we feel as something touching our body, then another related experience occurs. We begin to feel the currents of healing happening. That is to say, healing has very particular felt qualities. Because healing carries its own signature and is not a result brought about by something else, it is somewhat difficult to describe. The healing, however, is unmistakable: we feel the spiritual form of our body in the process of its being formed. It is as if the fabric of the universe itself is being woven with the material of the soul into a form unique to us. We inwardly realize that illness of any sort is "being-out-of-form," which can range from slight to gross. But this realization is a reflection after the fact, not something intrinsic to feeling the healing currents.

When we locate the healing currents within the other currents of Silence, we know it because our body feels just right, active currents of healing are present, and we feel the presence of bodily joy. We feel as if we are being held by a tender, loving, invisible presence. We may find it somewhat difficult to sustain this experience, as the currents of healing alternate with those of the invisible body of Silence, but as we become practiced in entering into the Silence we find it possible to sustain the healing experience longer. Mostly, we just want to stay in this place, but we can do so only when our attention is focused in the witness-consciousness just described. Usually, on a day following such experience, we feel more alive, not necessarily more energized, but more whole, because we now live the experience of being as much a part of the invisible worlds as we are of the visible. It is as if Silence has been invited back into every cell of our body. We have inwardly sensed that our body is not completely our own, and yet not an entity that exists completely separated from the world. It is, rather, completely interwoven with the world-currents of Silence.

Feeling more alive carries distinct qualities that differentiate this healing from other forms. Bodily joy is the primary characteristic: it is an enlivening, an inner knowing of what it is to be a spiritual-soul-bodily being. It is an experience of levity that also makes us realize that we have been living too much within the force of gravity. Symptoms may or may not be alleviated; if they are alleviated, the symptoms are typically not gone permanently after one or two or more meditative sessions with Silence. We are being introduced into a new way of living, rather than being taken to an inner clinic to have something removed. At this stage, what is most significant is simply feeling the wholeness and integrity of our body, belonging with the wholeness of invisible beings in the world.

When we have learned to enter witness-consciousness, are well acquainted with the experience of the healing currents, are comfortable moving attention around, and are sure that we have not switched from witness-consciousness to spectator ego-consciousness, we can move into a second aspect of the healing of Silence. We can scan the body using the spiritual act of attention and begin to allow Silence to come into specific bodily symptoms. Scanning is a simple matter of entering into the Silence, feeling the presence of the invisible body of Silence, and then shifting attention to the top part of the invisible body. This is the place from which scanning begins. Then we slowly move our attention down through the invisible body of Silence. As we do so, we come to places where the scanning no longer goes smoothly. We may become aware of bodily symptoms, often symptoms that we had not even recognized before. We may notice aches and pains, but more significantly, we may sense inner image-shadows that appear at various locations of the invisible body of Silence. These image-shadows are felt senses of places that are blocks, or materializations, within the invisible body. It is easier for us, at first, to work with the aches and pains.

When we come to a place of an ache or pain as we are scanning, we may notice that even with the attention that is behind or surrounding the ache or pain we can still feel the bodily joy that characterizes the ever-present currents of healing. When we let those currents of joy flood through the place of the pain, the pain disappears, at least momentarily. We feel as if it is dissolving. We employ the exact same procedure when we come to the places of shadow images, but since these places do not radiate pain, our experience of them as filled with healing currents through the act of attention is more subtle. We go on with scanning, following this method until we come to the region of our toes. Then we slowly open our eyes and sit in stillness for a few minutes. The healing currents have now been allowed to flow through the whole of the body. Some of the pains will simply be gone. Some will be gone, but return after a while. We can expect this, for the intention of this healing is not to seek eradication of symptoms but to enter into a new form of relating with the body.

We usually relate with our body as if it is an object, albeit a quite unusual kind of object, but we do not usually experience our body from within it. Our relationship with it is a peculiar one for we experience it as other than us, but we nonetheless completely identify ourselves with it. When we go to a medical doctor, we are introduced to this body that is other than us because in these days our own body experience is of very little interest to doctors. As part of modern medicine, doctors are interested in the body that can be measured, blood tests that can be done, heart rate that can measured, and x-rays that can be taken. This body is not the body of life, but the body of life as it is intermixed with the body of death. That is, our body in large measure consists of the dying away of life, the extrusion of material after the life-forces have been used up. But the material and visible aspects of the body are not the living body. The living body is invisible. We are much closer to the living body when we experience the invisible body of Silence. When we do so, we have moved to an experience of the body from within, *within*, not as inside the physical body but *within* as an inner witnessing presence to the ongoing form of the body as it is every moment being created. Our intention is to gradually extend this new experience of the body so that it becomes the more normal experience of incarnation.

When our experience of embodiment shifts to a sense of the living body, our relationship to symptoms changes drastically. Symptoms become for us unrecognized possibilities rather than indications of something gone wrong. They are aspects of the wholeness of the realm of Silence as this wholeness comes into relation with the particularity of our individuality. Symptoms then are the particular aspects of Silence that are not being allowed their full voice, or their full presence within the individuality of the spiritual beings that we are. Perceiving body symptoms in this way is so entirely unusual that it takes some time just to comprehend what is being stated here.

Silence is the medium that brings toward us a sense of our becoming, of our being within a field of destiny, and of an orientation from the future. Due to Silence, we are not simply the products of our past, the carriers and enactors of memory, nor the playthings of archetypal imagination. Our future, however, is not yet formed, not anywhere. The future is an open field of possibilities, and Silence is the Mother of possibility. When we feel the pull of the future from within Silence, we experience an orientation toward action within a field of openness in which we, in our spirit, are open to the harmonies of the universe. When we are unable to feel the pull, symptoms appear within the physical body as the expression of those possibilities. Working with the healing of Silence does not require us to interpret symptoms symbolically, but to return the symptoms to the wholeness of the Silence.

Symptoms are our greatest gift for guiding us toward our destiny. If, within Silence, we place our attention within a symptom, we experience a bodily sensation, a tendency toward movement, or a feeling. When we let these experiences form into images, they reveal that what is trying to pull us into action is an aspect of our destiny. Images are bridges between ordinary body consciousness and Silence, so when we *listen* to them from within Silence, rather than interpret them, we regain a sense of direction in our lives. We usually are not even aware that we do not have a good connection with our destiny.

Destiny is a particular feeling quality, not cognitive knowledge of what is going to happen to us in the future or what we are going to be or do. We feel it as being in harmony with the larger and more comprehensive forces of the universe. It is a distinct feeling, but one that disappears when we strongly feel symptoms, whether of a bodily nature or equally of a psychological nature. When we feel symptoms, our consciousness narrows, and it either focuses almost completely within the symptoms, if they are strong, or it subtly distracts us from the wholeness of consciousness. Thus it is not hard to understand the urgent feeling that symptoms are bad and to be gotten rid of. We do not realize that when we do so, we narrow the feeling of our destiny experience.

The purpose of working with symptoms by going into the Silence, by entering into the inner experience of the invisible form of our body, by scanning this form with the act of attention, by finding and entering symptoms with our attention, and then by simply inwardly listening, is to connect with our soul-spirit being. Symptoms have a strong material-like component and so we sense them as foreign to who we are, but that is because consciousness withdraws from them. A conscious effort is then required to fill them again with the presence of a consciousness that is both diffuse and quite specific at the same time. When symptoms are filled with Silence-awareness, we are able once again to be within the fullness of Silence.

There is no doubt that making the claim for symptom alleviation would entice many people into working with Silence. Such a claim, and indeed such a hope, produces a shrinking from the being of Silence right back into our own egotism. The intention of working with the healing of Silence is to provide us with an important means by which Silence can become a central and ongoing focus of our lives. And such a focus is for the sake of Silence, not for our immediate and direct benefit. Bringing symptoms into relation with Silence opens up the highly significant time current that has to do with our "becoming" and with how we can increasingly be of service to the spiritual realms.

TREMBLING UNDER A MASS *of stars: deeper and deeper. In a dream I am told that behind the heart there lies a tiny organ that, though totally unknown, is felt when it quivers in the echo of the first conscious Silence. Dreaming me says, "Oh, that time I crept outside to get away from everyone and their words, and I lay on the ground to hide from the sounds and find peace in the silence." Remembering the smell of grass, the snuffle of the dog's curious, wiggling warmth, the swaddling of the dark, silent night; here my heart leapt through my throat and into the heavens that offered the silent love of night.*

From that moment, there remains within my soul that which recognizes any silence; that comforts and consoles, holds and heals. This tiny organ of perception; the one just behind the heart; the one not spoken of or acknowledged: it is there in all of us; it trembles with joy when Silence approaches. We think we have butterflies in our stomach; but truly, we are sensing the approach of a tangible realm. It is a realm that we are hardly aware of, yet are desperately seeking. When we stumble onto it, it fills us with unspeakable wonder and we are awakened into the realm of our true human spirit.

— Cheryl Sanders-Sardello

CHAPTER 6

Silence in Daily Living

L ike all phenomena of a soul or spiritual nature, Silence quickly disappears as soon as we leave a contemplative or meditative state, whether we enter such consciousness through the happy circumstance of intimacy with natural or artistic settings or through conscious inner work. The world of our usual commerce is too strongly with us and anything of a subtle nature withdraws from the onslaught. Our functional lives demand a different, more focused, goal-oriented, and mental consciousness, and being constantly with the Silence would make our practical life difficult. Nonetheless, we can inwardly develop in such a manner that it becomes possible to enter into aspects of Silence anytime we wish and remain in full consciousness while fully present to the world and what we are doing. We can allow the ground of receptiveness into daily consciousness. How we do things then begins to change quite radically. We can live a life of Silence with the mindfulness of ritual.

In his book *The Quantum Mind and Healing*, Arnold Mindell presents an exercise, which I have found, when practiced regularly, develops the kind of soul flexibility that makes it possible to go into Silence in the midst of whatever we are doing and to perceive the world as wrapped in Silence. This practice is done to develop image-consciousness, which is a fully conscious capacity to perceive the world as image-qualities.

71

Image-consciousness is a bridging form of consciousness between our interior activity of Silence and our outer perceiving. It breaks through the limitations of perceiving outer things in strictly literal ways. Image-consciousness consists of perceiving in such a way that what is within us and what is before us are not sharply divided.

The exercise consists of closing our eyes and entering into the Silence as previously described. Once we can experience the currents of Silence, we practice developing this bridging form of consciousness. When we enter into the Silence with eyes closed and stay there, letting Silence pervade us, we always find it somewhat of a shock to conclude the meditation by opening our eyes. As we enter back into ordinary consciousness, the experience of the qualities of Silence quickly recedes. Yet we can notice that it takes an act of will to go from inner Silence to ordinary perception. We have to will our eyes to open and, in a split second, also let our will adjust to outer reality. It is this act of will that has to be softened, for it makes too great an abyss between the two realms of inner and outer reality when we open our eyes suddenly.

We can modify this usual procedure by opening our eyes extremely slowly at the end of our time in inner Silence, so that our eyelids remain partially closed, somewhat blurring our vision. We notice that when we perceive the world through that blurred, softened vision the world presents itself in image form. Something begins to appear in the world around us that attracts our attention. What appears, though, will not be objects or things as we usually know them, but a surface, a reflection or light, or some partial aspect of a thing. And such things will be filled with an unusual liveliness. When something presents itself in image form, we feel the relationship with what we perceive. Thus we do not experience such a sharp separation between our perceiving and what we perceive.

In this state, we do not know what we are seeing. For example, once after being within inner Silence, I slowly allowed my eyes to open, using the "soft will" to let my eyelids partially open and remain partially open. I let my attention go wherever it wanted to go. Something appeared. I did not know what I was seeing. It was somewhat shocking to be within the world of sensing and not know what I was seeing. I saw something that seemed to be a long, narrow, gray, living and moving thing. It seemed as if it might be a snake, but I let that conception go and simply tried to remain with what appeared. It stayed gray, round, thin, and moving, now approaching me. I felt as if something magical was happening in the world, for I was aware that whatever this living thing was, it was not independent of my consciousness. I was also aware that I was not simply making something up or having a fantasy. I was in a new and different reality, one that was very real and objectively present, but one that required that I bring to it the living presence of Silence for it to persist in consciousness.

I let this image reveal its possible meanings. I listened and allowed it to reveal its significance to me. Was the natural world letting me know how alive it is? Was something of the world of the shaman revealing itself? Was the inanimate world, at a deeper level, showing that it too is animate? I didn't hear a voice or anything literal, but I had an immediate inner knowing that I was in the presence of something of importance, something I have not consciously experienced before and would, if it appeared in usual rational consciousness, reject. But here it was, and I inwardly let go of the impulse to reject what it was revealing to me. When I did fully open my eyes and come back into ordinary consciousness, I saw that I was looking at a dead tree branch outside my window. But this perception is filled with what I already know, and the livingness of the branch that became perceivable in the Silence now receded.

The intention of doing this imaging practice for a few minutes daily is to develop a capacity that allows Silence into our ordinary consciousness. We will begin to perceive changes but only under the condition that we consciously intend to perceive the world bathed in Silence and that we slow down enough to be present to it. Each time we do the exercise something different will appear to our image-consciousness. It is not important that we interpret the meaning of what appears; in fact, that is an unnecessary distraction. We will, though, feel an urge to know what the image means, for this urge is our usual consciousness wanting to get back into the center of things. It is best ignored.

As Silence becomes more an ongoing aspect of our lives, our perception of things of the world, and of others, changes from one in which we perceive surfaces to one in which we perceive the soul qualities of what is around us. We no longer have the impression that there are only things and persons in the world and that each thing or person occupies its own space, separate from what is next to it. Instead, we live in a fluid medium rather than a world of separate entities. There are no "its" in a world diffused with Silence; there is only the holiness of the "thou." Our perceiving becomes a meeting. Once we have entered into this kind of experience, we realize that we had not previously perceived the depth of the world but only our own preconceptions of the world. Even more, we had not perceived the soul-presence of other people. We had unknowingly perceived others as objects and had, also unknowingly, been using other people solely as things upon which to project our own needs, desires, and fantasies. And in order to keep the illusion going, we had been allowing others to do the same to us. Without the presence of Silence, it is not possible truly to meet the world and other people.

When we perceive the Silence within everything, we find a complete absence of negative consciousness. It simply has no place within a world wrapped in Silence. There are, of course, negative-like silences, for Silence can, under certain conditions, be terrifying, deadly, hurtful, anger-filled, divisive, and cruel. In these instances, however, Silence does not itself convey these qualities; rather, the presence of fear has usurped the activity of Silence, and these negative-like qualities are then actual experiences of fear. If we have practiced linking the inner world of Silence with the outer world of appearances, we have, by virtue of that practice, eliminated the kinds of judgment that allows in fears. So long as we maintain this true sense of the Silence, the complete absence of anything negative will continue to characterize the way we perceive the Silence within. The full range of emotional and feeling life goes on when we have come to live more fully with Silence, but the inner evaluating that typically goes along with such experiences withdraws.

Some aspects of Silence as felt in daily living can be a strongly emotional reaction to something, a drawing toward or a moving away from something. Sometimes we experience a strong sadness, even grieve, but the quality of unconditional intimacy is never broken, and even these emotional qualities are miraculously without negativity. In the presence of Silence, our emotionality transforms into soul-feeling, a *being-with* feeling of intimacy.

We cannot speak of the intimacy of our Silence-filled connection with the world as a "positive" experience. This kind of evaluating polarizes the wholeness of image consciousness, so somewhere there is bound to be an equally illusionary "negative" experience lurking. Besides, we want to assiduously avoid the new-age mentality of everything as positive. In our intimate connection with the world in Silence, our ego is not excluded, and judgmental consciousness comes through the ego. But when we are fully conscious and in the presence of Silence, judgment is not present and ego is magically transformed. Since Silence is all-encompassing, nothing of our psychic make-up is left out. When Silence also pervades ego, we are able to carry out our more usual daily actions without our ego wanting to usurp the whole of our consciousness. Typically, our ego exists in fear because it exists by separation: "I am not this, I am not that, I want this, I need that, I am afraid I am not getting what I need," that sort of constant buzzing. Silence completely calms these fears through which ego exists. We do not lose a sense of individuality in Silence. In fact, it is enhanced. We do not enter into any kind of dimmed or trance state in Silence. In fact, we are more alert, more awake, and more present.

It is the unconscious aspects of the ego that typically keep us as spectators looking at the world instead of being with the world. What exists unconsciously is highly conscious activity in itself. The term unconscious refers to the perspective of the ego. As all depth psychology acknowledges, however, the contents of the so-called unconscious have their own modes of consciousness. It is these unconscious but very active aspects that are transformed in Silence. On the one hand, our ego, in its fear of the world, lives within the nonconscious fantasy of escaping the world, either by having power over it, or power over others, or by imagining itself as already spiritualized. On the other hand, our ego fears the very possibility of the reality of spirit, for then it would seemingly have no place at all. So ego coaxes us into believing that all the comfort imaginable, everything we will ever need or want, is present here in the earthly world and can be possessed. We live, within our ego consciousness, with a sense of complete self-sufficiency that denies the presence of the spiritual worlds. Silence transforms these two unconscious aspects of the ego, its fear of the earthly world and fear of the spirit world, for Silence takes fear away. Silence heals fear.

In Silence then, we still have the capacity of focusing, which characterizes the functioning and true purpose of ego-consciousness, but we also have the new capacity of diffuse and whole consciousness that characterizes soul-spirit consciousness. When these two forms of consciousness meld, the world is perceived as holy. When our ordinary perception combines with Silence, we perceive everything in its holiness. We perceive that the world and others have a liturgical quality. It is a holiness that we do not experience in a static form but do experience as something more than emotional sentiment.

The ever-present movement of the currents of Silence takes us into the world as dramatic performance, where it weaves polarities, opposites, and contradictions together in its active motion. When we perceive the world through Silence, the world reveals the utterly particular in tension with the deepest meaning of things around us. We have before us and within us breathtaking moments of perceiving some things—a rug, a chair, a person walking by, the leaves of a tree, cars on the street—in their absolute particularity accompanied by the emanation of a holy presence. We usually perceive things in terms of categories: just a rug, or a chair, or a person walking by, and so miss the presence of the individuating soul that reveals itself. In Silence, things resonate within our soul, and each thing is experienced as "mine" and as "autonomous" at the same time. This is the experience of true intimacy and mystery. Something is within "me" and yet is totally free and independent of me. Our ordinary consciousness cannot perceive in this way: it bifurcates our experience, and in our usual perceiving, things are either possessed by our consciousness or left "out there" alone, as independent, abstract objects.

The image-filled qualities of the world, which are perceived in and through Silence as holy, are further characterized by being filled with a subtle but unmistakable sense of anticipation. It is an anticipation that seems to belong to the things themselves rather than belonging to our inner state of being. This quality, more than any other of the qualities of the world perceived in Silence, such as relating, healing, intimacy, and clarity, makes Silence compelling. It is not the peace Silence brings to us that makes us want to move toward it, but this aspect of holy anticipation within the very things of the world! An anticipation of what? By whom? The answers are not given within the experience of Silence itself. The sense of anticipation is simply present and opens us to experience the world as on the way, as unfinished, as still in the process of being created, of coming into being, and as moving toward some unknown completion. Any sense we have of the world coming to an end is completely dispelled in Silence-filled perceiving. With this felt sense of anticipation, we realize that our soul-spirit participation in Silence enjoins us with the ongoing action of the world coming into being.

In Silence we have the immediate experience that all of the space within which the things of the world exist, gathers, envelops, and pervades everything completely with a kind of quiet urgency. We know what it is like when we have something to say that comes quite spontaneously, not thought out in advance. The instant before we speak is like the anticipation that characterizes perceiving the world in Silence. In perceiving through the depth of Silence, we come to discover the invisible body of the world, the spiritual flesh within which everything is nurtured into existence at every moment. And we discover ourselves in a new way: as participants in the great being of Silence. We are not detached observers of an independent phenomenon, for we exist within what we are observing. We not only exist, we are being changed, spiritually enlarged by our act of participant-observation.

As we come to live more and more within world-filled Silence, we live less within the usual polarity that oscillates between a focus on ourselves and a focus on the outer world. The two worlds of subjective experience and outer presence dissolve into one field through what Henry Corbin, in speaking of Sufi spirituality, calls *sympathetic union*. This field, though unified, is nonetheless highly articulated, sensible, and textured. When we incline toward Silence, resonance is set up within our heart, prompting an inclination of our heart to enter even further into the realm of Silence. We incline toward Silence, and Silence inclines toward us, spiritualizing our sensing so that the material world and something of the soul being of others becomes spiritually perceptible.

When I was in Australia several years ago, I met an artist, a painter, who has cultivated a highly differentiated presence to Silence through spending weeks at a time in the Outback. To one first stepping into the Outback, it looks like a vast presence of sameness. This artist said that he would be walking along, maybe for ten or twenty miles, and all of a sudden he would walk into a completely new region, in spite of the fact that to the ordinary eye there was no perceptible difference in the terrain. He was speaking of walking into a different region of Silence. The moment this happened he could perceive a difference within himself and a difference within the landscape. Each region of Silence, he said, has its own distinct qualities. Many of his paintings show the presence of a seemingly infinite number of beings within space. To me, these paintings express his creative perceiving of the Silence, not something that the vast presence of sameness made him imagine in a subjective way. These beings seem to be presences of the dead, as if Silence consists of the spiritual presence of the dead all around us. Looking at these paintings, we have the sense that the spiritual worlds are neither off in some other, higher region nor in the netherworlds but right here. While these particular paintings seem to express the Silence of certain regions of the Outback as the active presence of the dead, we cannot say that these presences characterize all of Silence. But the creative perception of this artist does begin to awaken our sense of Silence as a Who. Up to this point, we have imagined the "currents" of Silence as a way to understand that Silence is not a completely static presence of a unified kind. We can now more fully imagine these currents as spiritual presences, which do not inhabit Silence but are the essence of Silence.

We tame, sentimentalize, and crush the power of all that is around us by placing spiritual presences in the great Elsewhere: in deep outer space or into an imagined spiritual world or heaven or hell. These presences from Elsewhere occasionally grace us with a visit to reveal something of importance to us. They seem to be powerful servants who try to help at least some of us, or they seem to try to harm us. Either way, there is a vast gap between our earthly life and the worlds of spiritual or demonic beings. We imagine that there is a threshold separating the realms, and there may once have been such a threshold, as spiritual initiates have always spoken of one. Now, however, the threshold is dissolving. The world is pervaded with spiritual presences, and we brush against them each time we find the way into Silence.

Through Silence we begin to develop a "right" imagination of spiritual beings. We typically imagine such beings as entities, as some kind of ethereal presences that float around in spiritual worlds. But spiritual beings are not entities; they are individuating aspects of the Whole of Silence, of Silence as Whole. Our rational mind cannot comprehend such a notion; we have to experience it in the Silence itself. Within the medium of Silence, we find that there are not separated beings, some of whom, like the angels, send us messages and information from time to time. In Silence, the medium is the message.

Perceiving the world in Silence makes us think differently. We begin to be aware that our thinking about spiritual matters has been materialistic. It could be no other way because the form of our thinking has been formed, for all the years of our lives, within a completely materialistic framework. So when we begin to think about spiritual things, we do so with the same forms as we think of anything else. Silence, however, is being on the way to spiritualized thinking. The very form of our thinking has to be re-formed from "thinking about" to "thinking within," and Silence is the teacher. As our thinking about spiritual things gradually re-forms out of its accustomed ways, which reduce the subtle to the gross, our new thinking within helps us further refine our perceiving of the Silence. We can eventually get to where we don't have to set aside thinking in order to experience spiritual realities.

Thinking within the Silence is, of course, not at all brain-bound thinking. It is a spiritual act, which is possible only because such thinking also takes place within the Silence itself. Silence is intelligence. It is a mode, a form of intelligence. It is Wisdom. As we enter into Silence, we enter into Wisdom. We do not become wise but enter into the objective Wisdom of world processes. Judgment, as the primary mode of our thinking, ceases or is taken up only when needed for our practical life. As we enter into the Wisdom of Silence, we allow ourselves to be taught by the things of the world. We allow the revelations that flow from the Silence to give rise to their thinking through us. Such an apprehension of "new thinking" has its precedent in holistic science, alternative medicine, meditation, prayer, and even in such practical activities as architecture. For example, the great architect of light, Louis Kahn, was fond of saying that he works within the notion of letting the materials tell him what they want to be. While there are these and many other precedents for "thinking within," none have acknowledged the ground of their receptive intelligence as the Wisdom of Silence.

THE PATH LEADS *to a place of such presence we are suddenly able only to whisper. Then within moments we stop speaking altogether, for the presence is so thick we can only listen. Moving with all due caution, so as not to allow the matter on which we tread to speak of its nature and substance, we gentle our feet to the status of kittens and lift the weight out of them with each footfall. Ah, there it is: the being whose realm we have passed into. It is not the majestic trees, the twittering creatures, the passive moss and fern. They live here, but they are not why we slow our breathing until we are all but gasping for breath. We know we must utterly give ourselves over to the laws of this place. To be here requires attention, listening, and gazing deeply without assaulting each thing seen with a conclusion. The silence here is not just in the "what has been," it is most deliciously waiting, too, in the "what will be." Movement in the silence is toward, not away from. Press ever in to the waiting silence that holds all possibility. Ignore it at your peril, for otherwise life is a presumption, which is the home of disappointment.*

Entering the redwood forest, reverence takes hold of us through the silence of the mysterious presence. Of Silence.

— Cheryl Sanders-Sardello

CHAPTER 7

Making a Clearing for Silence

In order to live in an extended way within the presence of Silence, it is helpful to develop a practice of inner clearing. The clearing work is necessary because Silence is the activity of spiritual beings and spiritual life, and there are no death forces in Silence. Silence, for this reason, is life-renewing and healing. In our everyday lives, though, we are continually taking in death forces, which are found in everything that is already prepackaged, given to us as completed, and requiring us only to consume. Whether in the form of education, religion, media, work, products, and most everything else we are involved in, we are clearly immersed in death forces. The already completed and already known, when conveyed to us, deaden our soul and veil the liveliness of Silence. We constantly feel pressed by being fed the already known in attractive packages, as well as packages filled with fear. There is another source of death forces that is more subtle. Unless emotional life transforms into feeling life through immersion in Silence, emotions themselves are pervaded with death forces. The presence of what works against liveliness in emotion is difficult to understand, let alone experience. It seems that there is not enough emotion in the world, yet when we look at what rules the world, we see it is abstract cleverness and uncontained emotion.

Abstract cleverness devises the death forces of production and consumption, and uncontained emotion bursts through the confinements of what abstract cleverness builds and seems to offer life. In abstraction and emotion the energetic activity of our soul is being mistaken for the experience of life forces. Until we can fully feel what the life forces are like by developing an intimate connection with Silence, we will imagine that emotion is what we are looking for, and we will be subjected to the inevitable pattern of emotional upheaval followed by depletion. The depletion that follows strong emotion shows quite clearly that emotion does not give life, but the turbulence of emotion gives a semblance of life when all else is ruled by the abstractness of the head. Emotion then seems to be our way out. Emotion, however, is the polarity of abstractness and is not its solution, but it relies on the presence of the abstract for its subsistence. The more the world turns to the abstract, the stronger and more destructive uncontained emotion becomes. While we cannot avoid these two pervading forces of abstraction and emotion, we can unmask them for what they are and find the practical means of ensuring that they do not take over our newfound relationship with Silence.

The difference between emotional experience and the feeling life is that emotion occurs quite automatically as a reaction to something that happens to us. Someone may be angry with us and we react. Or someone acts lovingly or seductively and that evokes an emotional response. We are not free in our emotional life. Emotions simply come. We like some emotions and dislike others. Such responses come packaged as sympathy or antipathy. They are strongly connected with bodily experience.

As we grow into deeper relation with Silence, we begin to observe our emotional reactions. We find, for example, that we have a hard time recovering from the reverberations of strong, difficult emotional responses. It is as if we are weighed down in our soul and can't perceive the light. With emotional responses of a more pleasant nature, we find that it becomes somewhat difficult to perceive the inner qualities of soul, and instead we find ourselves bouncing along in the world, slightly high. The feeling life differs considerably from such emotional reaction. Feeling is a form of knowing rather than bodily reacting. Through feeling we are given access to the soul dimension of the world and of others; we have a sense of what is going on inside others and even within aspects of the world. Feeling is also more centered in the region of the heart. We are much more free in the realm of feeling than we are in the realm of emotion. We can hold feelings, though it is true that, given the added dimension of freedom, we can also withhold feelings.

If we have been immersed a long time in mass culture, we are not likely to be in very good connection with the feeling life. And we are much more prone to emotions because mass culture plays on emotions, seeking to invoke exactly the kind of emotions needed for continued mass consumption. Entering into Silence, we first have to push through a kind of emotional barrier that would keep us out of Silence. Once we have pushed through, our life of feeling develops dramatically. It is then more possible to work on clearing the soul.

Clearing the soul from the overload of death forces consists of releasing images of things that attach themselves to our soul. It is helpful for us to have a sense that when something of a prepackaged nature comes to us the packaging is like a Trojan horse. Filled with active forces of death, it comes in highly interesting, attractive, and desirable packages.

An easy exercise gives us an idea of what it is like to clear the soul by releasing images every day. On each of five small pieces of paper, we write one thing that we find occupies a recurring place in our imagination. It can be a relationship, a material thing, money, something we desire, something we do, or an emotion that we experience. We place these pieces of paper in a pile in front of us, go through each of them slowly, one by one, and let ourselves imagine that we are actually giving away the thing that we stated on the paper. We make an inner image of what is on each piece of paper, one at a time, and then release the image, letting it dissolve. We let ourselves inwardly feel what it is like to give that thing away, to not have it anymore, neither the fantasy of it nor the desire for it.

When we release something from its internal attachment to our soul, we may immediately experience deep sorrow or loss. This experience may surprise us, even shock us. But along with this experience of deep sorrow, we feel an opening of a round-like, small space deep within the region of our chest, in the region of the heart. We feel pulled toward this center. This feeling is extremely important as it directs us toward the place of purest Silence, the interior of the heart.

If we are perceptive in an inner way, we experience a second occurrence that is concurrent with feeling sorrow and loss. Light appears. This light may take a number of different forms: it may be bright, it may be more like an immediate memory of a light that suddenly gleamed and was gone before we could attend, or it may be more like a feeling of what light is like rather than an actual experience of light. Whatever its form, this inner light is actual and real and unmistakable. We do not experience this light, though, unless, when we give away what we have imaged, we strongly feel the release of something that is attached to our soul. The inner experience of light illuminates and also lightens us. For a few moments we distinctly feel lighter, not as inwardly heavy as we did the moment before.

Sometimes when we do this exercise and release something we feel the sorrow so strongly that the feeling overwhelms the light. We feel this sorrow in a very strong manner, for example, when we imagine releasing from the soul the image-presence of someone we love. We must then realize that we do not release the love, but only the inner image of the person that occupies our soul—the prepackaged notions that we carry concerning that person and may have carried for years. The image may carry a lot of emotion, but this emotion is not the love.

Clearing the soul for the sake of Silence is not to be confused with notions such as detachment or other notions from religious traditions, such as becoming "egoless." There are connections between inner clearing and the practices of religious traditions, particularly to the mystical tradition and initiatory practices, but our interest and concern are with developing practices of Silence that are suitable to contemporary conditions of soul life and that can be carried out in daily living.

Our challenge is to keep this first glimpse of the inner light open. We need to keep going and keep experiencing, but it is quite important that we not come to any conclusion. Let us not call the inner light God or say that this direction is the same as that of the mystics or that this fits into one system or another. The inner work of clearing involves returning again and again to this light and perhaps finding ways to strengthen it. Releasing the prepackaged world and our emotional energy becomes an ongoing process that we enter into and is not just a matter of stepping over a threshold. We come to a point where we recognize that the light is there all along, that it is always integral to the Silence itself. When we close our eyes and enter into Silence, it seems as if we are in darkness. However, this darkness is quite different from the absence of light, for it is a luminous darkness. Practicing this exercise helps quicken our sense of this luminosity of Silence.

The inner images of prepackaged things, events, and experiences that we have taken into the depths of soul life have had the effect of absorbing the luminosity of Silence. This inner experience of light is so slight and so momentary that it is immediately filled in. All that still lives within us from our past actions, experiences, and desires, which were not created out of our own individual soul-spirit being, and all of our ongoing experiences in the world fill it in. The inner light is a momentary experience of the creative light of Being. This opening to the light can be strengthened only by our conscious act of releasing something from the soul, not just once but in an ongoing way.

A variation of the previous exercise consists of doing a backward review of our lives. Starting with the present, we inwardly start moving back in time, trying to remember in image form the events and experiences of our lives, including especially those experiences that harmed others. It is not only mass culture that obscures the luminous darkness of Silence; even more, the tactics we have developed to project the difficulties of our lives onto others makes sensing this luminosity difficult. Once we have done the backward review of our lives, we can begin the practice of doing a backward review of the day each evening, going through the events of the day. We start with the first moment and work back, step by step, feeling the images and being particularly aware of how we have harmed others. It is extremely important, however, that we not judge ourselves and not dwell with those experiences in which we harmed others. If we linger with these images and ruminate on them, guilt is produced, which further blocks the luminosity.

Blocking the light of the soul results in a further need to attach to prepackaged things, ideas, and emotions, because they provide a semblance of light, a double of light. When the light is blocked, we develop the desire for things, not the Silence. Releasing things gives Silence a chance to strengthen, and gradually a time comes when our desire itself changes. It is not that we now desire the inner light instead of a big house or something or other; rather, our desire is turned inside out. Instead of desiring more things, stronger emotions, or something more to hold onto, we experience the desire of Silence. Our own desires have the quality of pushing us: we desire something or someone and, while we are drawn to what we desire, our internal experience is one of an impulse, an urge, or a compulsion. We feel the desire of Silence, however, as a gentle pull.

We begin to feel the desire of Silence once we attune to the luminosity of Silence, whether inwardly or in the world around us. This luminosity reveals that Silence is a place that is no-place, rather than merely a state of consciousness or the absence of sound. What is a place that is no-place? It is the experience of Silence as definite and placed and yet not located as "here" or "over there" in space. We feel drawn to a "kind of place" when we feel the desire of Silence. To describe Silence we have to resort to such unexplainable, but nonetheless very accurate, notions in order to defy what Henry Corbin calls the *agnostic reflex*. The agnostic reflex is the attempt on the part of our rationality to escape the reality of Silence by resorting to all sorts of explanations that try to reduce it to the already known.

We can certainly go into the Silence without the practice of clearing, and much of what we have said up until now can be experienced without clearing. But clearing brings to the forefront new qualities of Silence that transform our inclinations to work for ourselves in more or less selfish ways in to inclinations to be of service in the world. Within the close surround of Silence, we do not change what we may be doing in our work, our profession, or even the activities of daily life. Rather, what we do and how we act are bathed in the qualities of Silence's gentle pull.

Assent is one of the qualities of Silence that clearing brings to our work. Saying yes to whatever we do. Saying yes to the spiritual dimension of our being, even though in most instances we may not have a clear notion of the specific nature and content of the spiritual dimension. For example, we may install computer programs for businesses, sell insurance, or teach. When Silence plays more fully into our lives, such actions transform subtly but perceptibly from something that we do and feel in charge of and wholly responsible for into a response of assent from the reverent regions of Silence. Our individual attitude of assent resonates the essential quality of assent that inheres within Silence, and thus, if our soul has become receptive to Silence, we cannot help but live within this orientation of assent. The presence of assent diminishes any skepticism, self-doubt, hesitation, inertia, self-centeredness, or self-concern in what we do. Certainly elements of such qualities are still present, but they recede into the background and come forward only when we lose our connection with the Silence. We do not suddenly increase in confidence, not in the way motivational gurus usually speak of confidence as a strengthening of ego, for such confidence is an opposite of doubt, and Silence removes us from living in opposites. It is no longer a matter of our being either self-confident or filled with hesitation. We are filled with a companion-presence that guides us through our activities so that we perceive and act with love.

The quality of assent does not make us more skilled, self-confident, or better at what we do. It does not make us better materialists. The presence of this quality helps us to feel that no matter what we are doing, even those things that seem to completely lack any spiritual aspect, our soul senses something inward and moves toward elevating even the most mundane things of life. With this felt quality that comes from within Silence we creatively shape the expression of our actions, imbuing them with reverence. We feel that we are chosen to be of help to others in what we do. In the moment of assent, we make all our potentialities accessible so that the force of Silence can work through us. We lose our sense of reserve and caution, and relinquish our calculative mind that is seeking to get something out of our actions for ourselves. Assent is a creative act. It opens the inner heart space for something to be created rather than just performed.

When we have cleared a space for the presence of Silence to enter into whatever we are doing, we feel the presence of grace in our lives. When we have gotten to the point of feeling the desire of Silence and can call to heart that feeling when we are about to begin our day and our work, we feel graced. Grace is a second alteration of the soul that comes through the work of clearing. Grace is the permeation of our soul with divine love. It is a very palpable bodily feeling. It feels as if we are accompanied by a radiance, and in the midst of such radiance we radiate a glow. Sometimes others can even see or intuit the presence of this glow.

The presence of the grace of Silence is diffuse, soft, and yet brilliant. When we are graced, it is impossible to hold onto its presence for ourselves, for the nature of being graced is to grace others. The power of grace unblocks whatever is blocked. For example, we find ourselves able to speak things we have not been able to speak before. It is not that we didn't know these things or that we were hiding them, but without the presence of grace we have an essential inability to say what we feel or think or imagine that is of a spiritual nature. We tend to hold back, not letting that dimension of our inner experience into the world. We do not find words adequate to spiritual experience. With the presence of grace we do not become preachy, nor do we interpret what we do in terms of any kind of religious doctrine; rather, the hidden fullness of who we are and what we are doing becomes available. We now feel that we are overshadowed by the spirit-beings of love. This experience releases us from the kind of incessant self-examination we usually get caught up in.

Grace does not free us from our weaknesses and our suffering, but it does free us from the feeling that these difficulties make life complex. Grace brings a newfound sense of simplicity. Everything that seems complex and incomprehensible is taken over by grace and what seems complicated is solved. Through the presence of grace we know what is wanted of us and we are able to respond. Problems decrease in importance. They are still around, but they do not present themselves as limitations or obstacles. The kind of hesitation we are accustomed to feeling, as in "I could do this, if it weren't for that" simply does not seem to be present.

Our problems take their place within a larger context, where they are held in balance with their inherent possibilities and a deep centering sense of the spiritual nature of our actions.

We cannot control grace or make it happen, but it is very obvious to us when it is present. It is bestowed, but it requires the receptivity that we develop through our connection with Silence. Grace divests us from what seems to be ours, so the presence of grace is often accompanied by our sense of being less in control and of possessing nothing. As we continue to clear away what we feel are our private possessions, grace increases. Keeping our connection with Silence becomes crucial, then, because we can easily feel that we are losing our identity as we undergo a transformation of who we know ourselves to be. We begin to find, though, that we are carrying far more than what has been allotted to us to carry and that we have identified with that extra baggage. In large measure, we are fated to suffer the limitations of our bodily being, our circumstances, and our history, but this naturally given fate is accompanied by grace, the capacity to shape creatively and utilize our conditions to make something new. When, however, we take in and live according to what the prepackaged world gives, we lose our sense of being graced. We are then carrying things that do not belong to us, even though we have become convinced that we do.

Through our effort to clear away what may be blocking the Silence from full expression in our lives, we also develop a sense of the open hiddenness of this presence. We do not go around speaking of the benefits of entering into the Silence. We feel no inner urging to do so, and, in fact, doing so would feel to us like violating Silence. Rather, effacement, which is not self-effacement, becomes an important aspect of our lives. In this, we do not experience a stepping back from others or from what we do, we instead experience greater and deeper engagement, so that being of help to others simply through our presence becomes more important.

From our own presence alone we find that Silence frees others, and they may tell us that they feel freer around us than around other people. The "freedom" they feel is the soul presence of Silence. We do not hide this presence, but the essence of its being remains invisible. Silence, as it enters into our lives, remains veiled, and even if we wished to reveal it, we could not because its essence lies beyond language. Living within the presence of Silence is like living an esoteric practice openly.

Others may see us as calm, collected, and serene, and wonder about where our serenity comes from and how we got that way. We may even say that we spend time meditating or just being silent, but the essence of what is working through us remains concealed. This way of being is something we learn only by entering into it. It cannot be taught. It is beyond information.

The dazzling obscurity of the secret Silence outshines all brilliance with the intensity of its dark luminosity. Silence shines within us like the reflected image of the sun on a lake. We live within the depths of it, and it glows from our being. It is a liquefying power, an interiorizing power, a liberating power that frees us from the sterile hardness of dead, institutionalized forms, and brings renewal to the world. We are merely the carriers, the transporters of this great mystery, having dipped into it in the depths of contemplation. We bring from the depths some of this mysterious fluidity and offer it to the world. We are graced with the mantle of Silence and dissolve in its diffused brilliance. It opens the door to our heart.

SENSE FADES INTO NON-SENSE ... *language blurs to vaguely human noise. Is there really this much to talk about? Focusing on this conversation or that one over there, the relating of events of the most banal nature seems to take up the banner of proclamations!!!*

Then, straining to listen through the clamor, I find it. It has been there, permeating, lapping at the edges, scuffed up from the floor, held in place by furniture and knick-knacks. Good heavens! It's everywhere, even here, where it is most ardently banished. In trying to cover it up, chase it away, we've mostly just slipped through its borders like canoes on a river. All our noise cuts through the silence and whooshes right past. The silence is the water that holds up our boat, that our paddle pushes against, and that we glide through without taking notice unless we suddenly tip over, and are spilled out into the depth of silence when we fail to navigate correctly, or we are thrown off course by circumstances beyond our control. Then we enter unexpectedly (and most likely try to escape as quickly as we try to escape the water) into the foreign realm of silence.

What if we stayed for just a moment? What if we swam in the silence long enough to warm up to its temperature? Dive under.

— *Cheryl Sanders-Sardello*

CHAPTER 8

The Silence of the Heart

The way of Silence is the way of feeling, and the heart is the center of feeling. When we are able to place our attention into the center of the heart, we develop the cognition of Silence because feeling is a mode of knowing.

In all of the practices of Silence so far described, we feel the process of knowing to be very different from our usual ways of knowing. While in Silence, we are not thinking about anything outside the focus of Silence itself, although it is entirely possible to hold a thought within the currents of Silence. Our cognitive abilities are fully present. We are not in a trance, or in a dimmed state of consciousness; we are, in fact, more alert than we are in our ordinary thinking and perceiving. And if we deliberately introduce a thought, it finds its counterpart in the realm of Silence, and we are taken into the heart-essence of the thought.

Silence itself is pervaded with knowing. A kind of knowing lives inherently within the Silence and cannot be separated out as a "knowing about" something in the way that we, in our usual cognition as spectators, know about things from the outside. We are within a nonmental way of knowing, as if head and heart unite. Silence takes us into the heart, and similarly, if we place our attention into the interior of the heart, we are taken into Silence. Up till now we have not signified how central the heart is to the Silence.

To turn to the heart, we return again to the miraculous capacity of attention as the instrument for finding our way. Spiritual practices, when they do speak of the heart, are usually quite vague concerning what is meant. And while there are literally thousands of books on the spirituality of the heart, the heart usually equates with feeling that is not typically differentiated from sentimentality. In many instances heart and heart *chakra* are also equated. When we speak of the heart in Silence, however, we always mean the physical organ of the heart, unless speaking specifically of the heart chakra. The physical organ is highly unusual because it functions simultaneously as a physical, psychic, and spiritual organ. The history and iconography of the heart as physical and spiritual at the same time have been documented by Gail Godwin in *Heart* and by Louisa Young in *The Book of the Heart*.

When we speak of going into Silence, all along we have assumed that the heart is the instrument through which we perceive Silence and also through which Silence becomes individuated and cosmic at the same time. The heart is automatically enlivened in Silence and heart consciousness is the very liveliness of the Silence.

The development of our capacity to use attention to enter the Silence of the heart makes conscious the heart's spirituality. By *heart's spirituality* we mean that the heart functions both as the outer expression of the very form of Silence, with its chambers filled with the vortices of currents, and the very activity of Silence itself, as an infinite movement of inwardness. Heart's spirituality differs from a spirituality of the heart. There are traditions, particularly in Russian and Greek Orthodox religions, that give the heart a central place in worship. These, and other traditions, use the heart as the instrument through which religious practices, such as the prayer of the heart, take place. But these traditions do not focus on the inherent activity of the heart, which is already an act of a spiritual nature. For example, to contemplate Christ within the heart already relies on the heart's spirituality, so there are unexamined assumptions in this kind of contemplation. The main assumption is that the heart is capable of holding within it a spiritual presence because it is already spiritual in its nature and functioning. With attention within the Silence, the spiritual nature of the heart can be brought into feeling-consciousness with a much stronger vibration than we usually experience it.

When we engage in the practices of Silence, we are going to the heart's consciousness. We practice living within the activity of feeling, not the activity of having feelings but of locating the center of our consciousness within feeling. Heart consciousness and feeling are equivalent to each other. In usual consciousness, feeling is more vague than the clarity of thinking, but in heart awareness this is reversed. Feeling becomes intense and clear, while the cognition that is present does not dominate. We come to these revelations concerning the heart and Silence not by theorizing but from the immediacy of experiencing. It is possible to develop the consciousness of the heart. In doing so, we are able to enter into a remarkable intensity of Silence and become aware in a far more concentrated manner of the creativity, the healing, the devotion, and all the other qualities of Silence spoken of thus far. Through practices of the heart we become not just partakers of the gifts of Silence but also spiritual creators within this realm. We approach this awesome possibility with greatest reverence and humility for it is a creating act of our soul-spirit rather than an attempt to use the Silence of the heart to make something happen. Entering into the heart is a practice of entering the miraculous.

We first have to find our way into the interior of the heart with our attention. The research done by a group called HeartMath has made some inroads into developing heart consciousness, though the researchers do not go very far with it, and they tend to be very repetitive with their single insight. Nonetheless, they provide a quite helpful exercise for entering into the heart, which we use here in a modified form.

A question we initially hold regarding the heart is "How do we know that we have moved our consciousness from our head to our heart?" We can think that we have done this by being quiet and trying to center ourselves in the heart, but unless we have some kind of marker it is not possible to tell because even thinking about the heart entrains the heart to some degree. One exercise that helps to intensify our experience is to think of a conflict that we are currently undergoing or have recently gone through with someone. It need not be a serious or terribly turbulent conflict. We make an inner image of the scene and action of the conflict: the image of where we were, the presence of the other person who was with us, and what occurred. We let this image become as vivid as we can, undergoing the emotion again. Then we simply move our attention from that image to the center of our heart. Attention feels like an active current, and we can even feel it subtly move from the region of our head down the central line of our body to the heart. Moving attention is something very different from shifting thinking from one content to another; that is, we are not shifting our thinking about the conflict to one of thinking about the heart.

When our attention shifts in this manner, the presence of the imaged conflict disappears immediately, as does the emotion connected with it. The tension in our body, that contraction that comes with imagining the conflict, relaxes, and we drop into a different kind of space. After doing this practice for a while, we can then, in a relaxed state with eyes closed, practice shifting consciousness itself from its sensed location in the region of our head to the interior of our heart.

After doing this little exercise for some time and becoming accustomed to the difference between head and heart consciousness, we can use our attention to go directly to the interior of the heart at any time. When we first try this, we may notice our attention going to the region around the heart rather than into the interior of the heart. It helps to begin by being still and concentrating in such a way that the scattering of our usual consciousness begins to focus along a line that moves from the top of the head downward, a line that is in the center and toward the front of the body. The energetic activities of the body and its various organs are typically very scattered, as is our attention. These scattered activities spread throughout the body and into the many things we are doing, as well as into our thoughts, images, fantasies, and memories. To move consciousness to the interior of the heart requires strong forces of attention, so our attention has to be gathered into this more concentrated form.

We know we are still thinking of the heart in spectator consciousness, rather than being within the heart, if our sense of the interior of the heart, or the images that we experience as we move our attention there, are of the heart as a physical organ that we have come to know about through medicine and anatomy. The physical heart is where we do move our attention, but it is to the interior of the physical heart. And as soon as we have enacted the kind of consciousness that can so move, we have entered into inward, interior consciousness and have moved out of spectator consciousness. We physically feel the physical heart within this kind of consciousness, but we do not have the visual bias of a spectator consciousness.

Upon moving our attention, the first thing we notice is that we can feel the presence of our heart within our breast. It feels like a center of sensations of feeling, but objectless, with no attachment to some person or to a spiritual presence. We are within the action of pure feeling. We feel a slight tug at the place of the heart, a slight sense of expansion, and equally a sense of currents emanating from the heart. It is as if our heart is being touched. It is as if our heart glows. It is extremely helpful to simply practice moving our attention from our head to our heart and seeing how long we can remain within the heart-feeling we experience once our attention has shifted. Such a practice makes it possible for us to shift into the place of the heart in a split second in the more ordinary circumstances of life. Within the heart center we learn to listen to others without feeling an urge to respond, to just be a heart-presence with them. Such listening lets others enter and be held within our heart in a way entirely different than the heart-feeling of romance. It is our capacity to feel the soul-being of another person.

Once we can feel the feeling-presence of the heart and find that place at will, we can practice sustaining attention in the very center of our heart. Aligning our attention to the presence of the heart and then moving into the interior of the heart—in that sequence—ensures that we are not concocting a fantasy of being within the heart. Feeling the presence of the heart within our breast is a sensory experience that keeps this practice embodied. In this practice we move from the heart in its physical aspect to the heart in its soul and spirit aspect. But it is the same heart, only now experienced in its interior dimensions. It is a way to heal the split conception we have of the heart, but we must do so. On the one hand, we conceive of the heart as a physical organ that shoves blood around the body like a pump. On the other hand, we conceive of the heart as the center of feeling, joy, and love. The former conception of heart is of a substance without metaphor, whereas the latter is of a metaphor without substance. The heart, though, is a dual purpose organ, simultaneously physical and spiritual.

In the interior space of the heart, we feel all Silence intensified and compacted, not as a visual space arrayed before us but as an intimate infinity we are within. We feel the strange and contradictory experience of intimacy without something or someone attached to that intimacy.

Pure intimacy. Closeness of feeling. Warmth. Sometimes so warm our whole body begins to sweat. We feel a further contradiction. While intimacy implies a contained closeness, which is certainly experienced in the heart when our attention is there, it is not possible at the same time to find the boundaries of the space we are within. We feel the intimacy as endless. We feel that we are being held by what we are within. Yet we have no sense of an inside and an outside, so the experience of being held is purely an inner experience, a qualitative aspect of the intimacy.

While heart interiority consists of inwardness, it is a radiating inwardness that does not close in on itself. Thus the heart is the organ for perceiving interiority, the infinite region of our own interiority, and the pure interiority that defines Silence. While there, we feel quickened and enlivened, as if we are within the wellspring of life itself. A rather unusual, remarkable, and relatively unknown mystic of the nineteenth century, Jacob Lorber, gives a meditative practice that is oriented toward prayerfully acknowledging the center of the heart as the wellspring of life. He suggests moving attention into the interior of the heart and while there "looking" around until we find a small, tiny lump, a mere spot. This spot is the most unassuming aspect of the whole body but nonetheless the place from which the entire body is animated. I do not think he is speaking of looking around in a visual manner, for we are now in the region of pure feeling. Everything done within this region is a feeling-act that is nonetheless, in its own way, cognitive. So this place is something that we feel, but its feeling quality is of a most unassuming interruption within the vastness of interiority.

When we try to feel this spot within the heart, we must recognize that to feel within the heart we must actively create what we are feeling. We have to be in a mode of creative consciousness. That is not to say that we make up or invent this spot within the heart, for we are not in the mode of fantasizing. The interior of the heart is what Henry Corbin, the scholar of the great Sufi mystic Ibin Arabi, calls the *Mundus Imaginalis*. We enter into the imaginal world. It is a very real world, this world of feeling, but what goes on within it we can perceive only through the imagination of the heart. When we are within the heart, we are no longer in the literal world. We are in the world as given in imagination, so everything that we are conscious of is imagined yet objectively real. When, for example, we move attention around within the interior space of the heart and come to this little spot, we are imagining the spot. But we know the imagining is real when it is feeling-filled. Corbin uses the Sufi term *Himma* to describe the power of the heart's feeling-imagination. Himma simultaneously signifies heart meditating, conceiving, imagining, feeling, and ardently desiring. When we are within the interior of the heart, we are engaged in these acts from the point of view of the heart, which is not our usual conceptual understanding of these terms.

When we come with reverence to this unprepossessing spot of the interior heart and give thanks for the life being received, we feel as if we are kneeling at an altar, feeling the presence of the Divine within us. We feel this life we live flowing from divine life. As Divine presence comes into this most insignificant spot, it takes on an independent life. It is as if the Divine Being does not want to draw attention to itself because to do so would break its gift of freedom, making us bow in adoration every moment of our existence. Instead, it is possible for us to take the life we are given every moment in complete forgetfulness and still freely turn to give thanks at this meeting place of the physical with our psychic being. At such a moment we feel an awakening of every cell of our body, a waking up of our body into illumination, a spiritualizing of our body as a result of the feeling-cognition of the Divine within us.

The interior space of the heart is not empty space. It is composed of the currents of Silence and it recomposes them in accordance with each current's individuality. Our primary feeling of this active space is deep reverence. This experience of the interior of the heart is the other side of the physical heart; that is, it is the experience of the very life of the heart rather than something only of a material nature. Esotericists call this the *etheric* heart. The reverence we experience in heart's interior does not come from our personality, as if we have just walked into a holy place and feel we are supposed to act reverently. Within heart's interiority the qualities of reverence inhere, perhaps due to its union with the presences of the spiritual worlds.

From working with the heart for years now, I have come to feel that there are three aspects of the heart's spirituality: The heart lives in service. The heart lives in healing. The heart lives in worship. These are the three inherent activities of the heart. They are the primary currents of Silence that together constitute reverence. They are the actions that belong to and constitute the deep meanings of the word *heart*. Their actions do not originate from our thinking but are embodied actions of this organ that is body, soul, and spirit all in one. Constituting the primary currents of Silence, they, together, generate another force, which is properly called *projection*.

There are two senses of the word *projection*. We are now familiar with the psychological process of projection from the depth psychology of Jung. This sense of projection means that some unrecognized, unconscious aspect of our psyche, particularly the Shadow, is kept unconscious by our projecting it onto others. Projection in regard to Silence is something different and refers to the culmination of the alchemical process. In alchemy, when interior transformation has come to the point where gold can be created from lead, the interior power of this transformation projects outward, and whatever the projection touches transmutes into gold. The spiritual alchemy of the heart involves this kind of projecting. It belongs to the very nature of the heart to project its activity into the space around it. When we develop the capacity of heart-consciousness, the heart does not constrain or hold in what we image and feel there. The reverence of the heart's consciousness, which we feel, does not remain private. It becomes a countenance that projects into the world.

The heart's action of projection turns all that happens within the Silence into practical actions in the world. The subtle currents of the individuated Silence of the heart emanate into the world. We can quite easily experience these currents happening and need not rely on belief and hope that somehow the work of the heart is of practical value in the world. We can take a small bell or a chime, for instance, and with eyes closed ring it three times, leaving an interval of a minute or so between each ring. We then follow the sound from our ear out to the source of the sound, the rung chime. That is, we reverse the usual process of hearing that simply receives sound and attend instead to the active aspect of sensing. Each time we ring the chime, we let our hearing-consciousness ray out to the sound and then follow the sound current back to our ears. We begin to feel an awareness of a relationship between our inner being and our perception. We can now focus on the relationship itself, on the current that runs between the source of the sound and our ears. Then, as we inwardly form a picture of the currents, we make this picture into the form of a clear vessel of sound-current, like an alchemical vessel. But we do not imagine glass, we make sure the vessel is composed of the sound currents. Then, when we have the vessel imagined, we take it into the region of our heart and let our heart be at the center of it. We can feel the presence of the sound-current vessel holding the heart. After a few minutes, we use our attention to erase the vessel. We then open our eyes and notice our surroundings. Everything around us will be bathed in the reverence of Silence. Everything will glow, including the space between things. And we will feel ourselves as belonging to everything and feel spiritual presences around us.

This sensory awareness exercise is a way to imbue sensory experience with the conscious, individuated, intensified currents of Silence. Even though the exercise works with sound, the *synesthesia*—the coming together of all the senses within the interior body—means that our sensing as a whole amplifies within Silence. Upon opening our eyes, we can feel a haunting presence of Silence. It is there all the time, but it only comes forward and projects when we approach it reverently. The interior space we are within as we do the exercise transforms into holy space. If we are with others, we have a tendency to whisper, internally acknowledging that the Silence will immediately recede if we enter ordinary consciousness rapidly. Colors become vivid but not garish, as if illumined from within. The space between things and between the body and things becomes as if perceptible. We realize that color is light, not paint, because the walls and the things of a room change slightly in hue with the slightest change of light.

At first, the intensity of the heart-projected Silence does not last very long, but the length can be considerably prolonged just by our being quiet. If we do this sensory-awareness exercise regularly, the duration increases. Even when it fades and is no longer perceptible, the feeling of its presence persists. And if we take up the exercise as a kind of inner training after a while we can place attention in the center of the heart and perceive the projecting heart-Silence without first going through the exercise.

When we have established heart intimacy at a high enough level that we feel the desire of the Silence, and our desire to get something out of going into the Silence recedes, it is time to focus in the opposite direction. Instead of projecting the Silence outward where it meets with the World Wisdom of Silence, we move the world inward in a conscious process of individuating World Silence. The two movements always imply each other; the difference is a matter of focusing attention. As an initial exercise we can take any object we like, place it in front of us at a comfortable

distance, and simply perceive it as we usually do. Then we let our perceiving become more peripheral and diffuse, so that we are perceiving
the object in a less focused way while being present to as much of the
surrounding as we can. We practice perceiving the object in a focused
way for a few minutes, then switch to perceiving in a diffuse way. After
doing the alternating perception for several minutes, we try to perceive
both ways simultaneously. When we perceive both ways simultaneously,
we are present to the object-as-image. This visual awareness exercise, in
fact, is a variation of the sound awareness exercise. It is helpful to do this
practice until we can do it easily, but that may take several weeks of a
few minutes each day.

Once this new way of focused-diffused perceiving is established, we
can begin to perceive others in this manner. Our capacity to hold someone within our heart is based upon this kind of perceiving. If we simply
try to hold someone in our heart, we are working with an outer image and
idea of the person, not the person's actual presence. When we perceive
others in this new way, we are already present to them at the level of the
soul.

With this kind of fuller sensing, it is possible to be with another person and to hold the inner image of that person within the center of the
heart. When we perceive in this focused-diffused way, we find that our
preconceptions of the person disappear. In highly focused perceiving we
conceptualize the person we are with, without realizing that conceptu-
alizing is mixing in with our perceiving. Thus we perceive the physical
presence of the person while cognizing this person as nice, friendly, or
hostile; or as a teacher, a parent, a wife, a husband, along with a myriad of
other thoughts and images that dim the inner perceiving. When we are
more sense-present, these concepts recede. Then it is possible to make
and hold an inner image of this person. The other person senses being seen
in this different way. A warmth is felt, a feeling of truly being seen, a

knowing that there is a complete absence of judgment. And Silence pervades the meeting, so a strong sensing of reverence occurs. Most of all, this kind of perceiving, which holds the person within the heart-currents of Silence, frees the other person, who inwardly knows then what it is to be a free being, a spiritual being.

When we hold another within the Silence of our heart, the division—the split between perceiving myself "here" and the other person "over there"—dissolves because we now perceive a unified field. This kind of presence is what the poet Novalis means in the aphorism "I am you." Working with Silence in this way, we see that freedom cannot be felt on our own. To be in freedom, we need one another just as we do the unifying presence of Silence, but we need one another in a completely non-needy way. Freedom comes though the presence of community; it is not something that we can attain individually. Community, however, does not mean established and institutional forms, for in Silence community forms within the moment of meeting. And it continues: distance has nothing to do with its existence nor has even knowing a person in his or her personality.

When we feel practiced in perceiving others more wholly within the surrounds of the particular contexts in which we meet them, and we have further learned to hold the inner image of the person within our heart, it becomes possible for us to hold the person within our heart regardless of whether that person is present or not. It is, however, important that we carefully make an image of that person within heart-consciousness and not just feel that we are holding the person in our heart. Then, even at a distance, the person will feel something. We are not practicing some sort of distance communication experiment, though, so it does no good to call the other person and ask if he or she felt what we were doing at 10:00 a.m. That procedure would be trying to get spiritual relationship to conform to material relating. But when another person is in some sort of difficulty or in pain and we hold that person within our heart, that person finds inner capacities to meet his or her difficulties with inner presence and strength. Many people who have done this practice of imaging and holding within Silence for years have noted frequent instances of healing.

In a space *of absolute silence. Absolute darkness. Absolute emptiness. When time stands still. While even breath ceases.*

Nothing gives any hint of its accidental intention, so there is no way to know what is. I only know that every thing is some thing, and that nothing is not. Holding my breath, I know that in a split second I will lose this inner belonging and be thrown back into the ordinary separation between me here and everything else as other over there. Already, with this thought the singularity dissolves, and I know all that fills emptiness, darkness, silence, and time measured by my very breath and heartbeat has a name and a definition. Thus it moves away from me, becomes other than the experience of me here.

What if I could stay? Staying in the activity of the unity, not just the memory of the unity. Here, I would recognize that there is a point at which, even with the wholeness of a body, I can permeate solitude (the communion in space), darkness (the offering of the light), the measure of time (the transubstantiation of the living body), and even Silence (the proclamation of the creative word).

Thus Novalis says, "I am you."

— *Cheryl Sanders-Sardello*

CHAPTER 9

Silence, Prayer, and Meditation

We have been attempting to establish the world as the temple of Silence. If we can do so, we can enter Silence at any time through an act of attention and approach it in more active ways. By engaging in practices that strengthen our own inner presence as spiritual beings, we will approach others as spiritual beings. We can use all of the practices spoken of in this writing to develop our spiritual aspect, rather than simply doing things of a spiritual nature.

We locate ourselves as spiritual beings through the heart where we come into union with the vast spiritual being who is Silence. As we become quiet and receptive to the Silence, we let ego-consciousness recede and rest within our attention, or our spirit-selves. We then begin to speak within the Silence, speak in an inner way that constitutes praying, which is the proper mode of conversing within Silence without breaking the Silence. Praying then seems to be something that we do in much the same way that we have a conversation with another person. Instead of it being another person, though, we establish a relationship with a spiritual being, an angel, saint, Christ, Mary, or God.

When we look at prayers that have been formulated, they all have this characteristic of being an address to someone. They seem to be a recitation, whether in a vocal way or silent, of words addressed to a spiritual being. When we make up our own prayers, it seems as if we are addressing someone who is invisible, whom we nonetheless believe to be present and able to hear what we are saying. Prayer, though, is not really ordinary conversation; rather, it is conversation that takes place in an explicit way through the depth of the Silence. The form of prayer now being asked of us is from a consciousness entirely different from ordinary consciousness. It asks us to pray from the center of our spirit-being. To do so involves entering deeply into the Silence. In previous times, when ego-consciousness was not so intense, it was sufficient to ensure soul's engagement by simply praying. Now we are much further away from soul life, and we must actively enter into it in a conscious manner. Otherwise, our praying is wholly ego-bound.

We do not attempt to make this kind of prayer happen. The description that follows helps us recognize small and significant aspects of what may be happening, so that we can form a picture that restores liveliness to praying and so that others may make their own attempts and experiments to add to this account.

When we enter into the Silence deeper than ever before and find there the interior of the heart, then we inwardly speak a prayer. In more usual forms of praying, it is as if we are talking while never sure than anyone is listening. It is as if our words go out into the cosmos. Praying within Silence has different qualities. Each word becomes palpably interwoven with the Silence in such a manner that we feel as if the words are not being spoken inwardly by us but are aspects of the very fabric of Silence. The words become like images. They do not evoke images, but we experience the very words themselves as if they were spreading out in space, like the formation of crystals on a window in winter. The words lose the linearity of a spoken sentence and form into a whole pattern within the Silence, a pattern that is not seen but felt. The known content of the prayer begins to recede and each word becomes a world. It is then entirely possible to become lost within each word, so we have to be present enough in attention to move from one word to the next. Words spoken in prayer while we are in ordinary consciousness are linear, perhaps emotion-filled. These same words spoken while we are within Silence reverberate and resound, their resonance spreading out within the infinity of intimate Silence.

Praying can be mechanical when we thoughtlessly say words, but when we are more present to what we are saying, in an inner way, words form a to-and-fro relationship. The words resonate into the Silence, and the Silence immeasurably deepens the words spoken. The words of a prayer and what occurs in the field of Silence are not external to each other. We experience them as a word-silence field, which is a gestalt, a whole with two different aspects—word and resonance—rather than the two separate acts of the wording and the moving currents of Silence. Praying becomes a miraculous experience when we are able to be within the reverberating field rather than when we focus only on the prayer-words we are saying.

One way of making this experience more clear is to say a word of the prayer and then wait in the Silence. Almost immediately we feel the presence of the word reverberating within the Silence. Then we say the next word and wait. As our praying continues, the linearity dissolves, and we are within the felt presence of a creative act that both includes us and encompasses us. The words echo in an inner way as we silently speak the outer words. In this echoing we can feel, if we pay attention, an incredible, seemingly unending depth in what we are saying. It is as if we have entered a place where the word has become a spirit. The flatness of speaking transforms into dimensional space. This depth can extend to the point that the words seem to be no longer coming from "me" as I know myself to be but from a being within me that speaks. When we pray, it is as if a second person is within us praying at a depth we can hardly imagine. Through our presence within the Silence, our spirit-being is able to speak. When we pray in the more usual way, we are often not present with our spirit. The presence of Silence is necessary for our inner spirits voice to resound.

With this kind of praying, prayer and meditation join as one. Ordinarily, prayer, at its greatest depth, is an act of the soul. We say words and they reverberate within the depth of the soul. But we are more often than not unconscious of the reverberation. When we speak in the Silence with the kind of attention just described, our soul prayer hears an even deeper reverberating, and we find ourselves moved into the interior of the word, into the spirit of the word. We do not see spiritual beings, but the words themselves become filled with reverence, a reverence that is not ours but seems to belong to the very nature of the words. Silence, we have said, is pure interiority. When we pray, we discover a further interiority. We experience being inside the inside. Such deep interiority is felt at the same time as hugely expansive, as if we were within the interior of the cosmos.

The repetition that often characterizes praying, saying the same prayer over and over, imitates, at a literal level, what is already occurring at the level of the soul and spirit in union with Silence. However, in the Silence repetition is not linear; it is as if a vast chorus of beings is saying the words in symphonic harmony, intensifying the prayer while spreading it out into a spiritual universe.

When we repeat a prayer over and over, something far more goes on than repetition of the words. The ordinary world from which we speak the prayer and the soul and the spirit worlds into which our speaking reverberates echo back into the prayer, each with its own texture and landscape. In this kind of praying, these worlds are brought into a harmonious resounding whole. We feel an immensity while praying, we concentrate completely, and we know ourselves to be fully embodied.

We do not experience each of these aspects separately. We feel as if we have been formed into a new being consisting of the harmonious tonality of our body, soul, and spirit.

From the viewpoint of our ordinary consciousness, repeating words over and over again is boring and frustrating, and word meanings seem to go in circles, in fact, in the same circle. From within Silence, however, repetition is not circular. We step into depth only to find there is more depth, and more depth, and more depth, with each prayerful speaking, creating the next level of depth. Thus praying is a creative act, and when we are within prayer in this way, our experience is much the same as when we are doing any other creative act, such as painting or playing music.

Creating is never making something out of nothing: it is a mode of perceiving. When a painter creates a picture, in some sense the picture is already there, and painting really involves finding that picture through a creative act. That is why, for example, a painter can know when a wrong stroke has been made. The creative act of prayer uses interior words as the creative medium through which the spiritual worlds of the words are found. The words are like brush strokes, and we can similarly know, while praying, when we have made a wrong stroke. We often find ourselves going back and interiorly saying the word we have just said in order to find the right field of resonance. We may not know in advance where we are going in prayer, but it is very clear when we have lost the way.

A further aspect of repetition that occurs in praying within the depths of Silence is that in such repetitions we are progressively dissolving our usual, analytic mode of consciousness. We are working against all that is within us that wants to have explanations, wants to know what is going on, and wants to be in control. In fact, we bring a problem or a difficulty in life to prayer, not to get a literal answer or even to get a solution but to take this hard-edged, impenetrable difficulty and put it into a medium where it will dissolve. Many of the difficulties we experience have to do with the way we approach our different life circumstances. Our approach is probably analytical, and we have come up against something that defies an analytic attitude so we don't know what to do. Under these circumstances it is salutary to enter into the Silence and pray, over and over repetitively.

We usually pray for something. We are asking for help with a difficult circumstance in our lives, or we need something, or we pray for someone else. We also pray as a way of speaking with the spiritual worlds. When praying within the Silence, we find the speaking itself is all that is important. The initial intention drops away. It is like going to a symphony expecting to get pleasure from it, but upon entering into the symphonic sound we find there is only the music and no reason for being there except for the music itself. We no longer feel we need to receive something from what we are doing and, while praying, we even lose the usual sense of knowing whom we are speaking with. That is, we may begin praying to a specific being, but when we enter into the interior of the words, our sense of addressing someone who is somewhere else disappears. The words, in this deep way of being within their own interior, contain the intention, the speaking, and the one being spoken with, all within themselves.

Words of prayer resonate the Silence, and Silence in turn enlivens the inner gesturing of speech so that we can feel the creative element extending into the depths of our body. The words we speak in prayer begin to become more sensuous, even erotic. As we are speaking, even if silently, our words no longer feel centered in the head but in our whole body, as if our body has become a sonorous instrument. In this moment our soul embraces our body, and we are lifted but not separated from the materiality of our being, lifted into a silent body of love. As we deepen our praying, our presence within the tonal quality of the words that we are saying begins to come into the foreground while the content element of the words, though not disappearing, moves more into the background.

Our sonorous body, permeated with the living currents of the Silence of prayer, is like a musical instrument. We bodily experience the particular configurations of the currents of Silence specific to any given prayer, and we are, in such moments, pure acts of praise ringing out into the world. Praying in this way is, however, also an act of sacrifice. We have to relinquish for a time our usual capacities and capabilities to undergo a kind of transubstantiation of our being. We relinquish our usual powers of sensing and knowing and acting. This element of sacrifice is crucial, for otherwise we are engaging in an act that is ultimately self-centered. The process of praying initially moves us out of our self-centeredness, and it is only as we become more accustomed to praying in this way that our self-centeredness re-enters. We slip back into spectator consciousness and find ourselves wanting to get something for ourselves out of praying. Becoming aware of the element of sacrifice in our praying helps keep us from falling back into an egotistic sense of praying. In prayer we offer our usual capacities as a gift to the spiritual worlds, not reluctantly, but filled with the warmth of love.

In sacrificing our capacities, we are engaging in a reverse creation, taking what has unfolded within us in time and giving it to the timeless. Praying in this way is an act of creation. It makes a new Heaven and a new Earth. Such an imagination is entirely different from that of praying as a mode of communication between ourselves and the gods. The hermetic dictum "As above, so below" is reversed: "As below, so above." We cannot offer the spiritual worlds anything material, however, because that would be spiritual materialism. But we can offer the spiritual worlds the love that we are and the love that we have for others. Praying within the Silence is a purifying process in which love, the very essence of our being, is extracted and offered to the spiritual worlds.

When we pray, we are giving over our forces to the spiritual worlds in an act of love. The angels, spirits, saints, and the dead are fructified by our praying, for it establishes a relationship with them on their own terms, according to the ways in which those worlds operate. When we enter into the Silence and pray, it becomes self-evident that praying is not something that we do for ourselves, even if it does start out that way. Yet something from praying does enter back into our daily lives, something connected with the intent we began with. But the usual way of imagining this line of connection, which is a kind of cause-and-effect imagination, does not fit the experience here.

Does this mean that we avoid praying for help or praying for others? To work in the right way with these questions we have to remain true to our experience. We still do pray for help and for others. And we become acutely aware of the instantaneous way in which our praying brings about a difference. When, for example, I pray for someone who has been injured, I may begin with the intention of praying for that person. As Silence is entered and the words of prayer are felt from within the Silence, there comes a moment when all of my known powers go away. It is like coming to a place of utter desperation. It is the moment of sacrifice, which is something suffered rather than actively sought. At that very moment, within the currents of Silence, I feel blanketed in comfort. My body relaxes and I receive the knowledge that the person whom I pray for is also blanketed in comfort. I do not need to check with the other person to see if this has literally happened for it may not be conscious, but it has happened. That fact is given within the experience itself.

What is the source of this comfort? We feel it as an objective presence rather than an interior psychological state. The comfort is itself a spiritual companion-presence. When we pray and listen closely to the music of the words playing through our body, we have the distinct feeling that we are not alone in the prayer but with a chorus joined in singing.

We have to be fairly astute to detect this chorus since it is so unified it is almost like one voice. We also have to be able to place the content of our words in the background and pay more attention to the tones resonating through the body. Then we will hear this rather astounding quality that shows us that we are joined by an invisible chorus. It is this invisible chorus that is the comforter.

We do not pray alone but as a community of spiritual beings whose very existence must be that of praying. We should not take this in a narrowly literal sense. If we pray the Our Father or the Our Mother or the Hail Mary, or if we improvise a prayer, we don't have the sense that the community of the praying that we join is somewhere reciting these same words. That kind of imagination makes the spiritual worlds into a version of the material world. Rather, through speaking prayer within Silence and letting the rhythm and the tone and the imaginal quality of the words resonate within the body, we join with presences beyond ourselves.

The comfort that appears when we pray within Silence is a powerful force. We feel held by a completely loving and understanding presence, which has the power of removing all fear and anguish. Such praying does not take away what we are given to bear, but the way we bear it radically changes. Instead of a burden of heaviness, the difficulty has been lifted into the light. The task we are now given is to remember this light. But we are not restored to where we were before the difficulty arose, nor are others for whom we pray restored to where they were before. When praying ceases, we may still feel fear, but it no longer dominates and has no power over us. In fact, we feel joy, even though we still have the difficulty and the person we pray for may still be in danger, hurting, or in pain. This joy is not an emotion but the very nature of the comforting community of prayer. No matter how difficult things are, this sense of the power of comfort persists.

SELECTED BIBLIOGRAPHY

Athanasius of Alexandria. *Life of St. Antony,* in *A Select Library of Nicene and Post Nicene Fathers of the Christian Church.* New York: Scribners, 1890.

Childre, Doc and Martin, Howard. *The HeartMath Solution.* San Francisco: Harper SanFrancisco, 2000.

Corbin, Henry. *Alone with the Alone.* Princeton: Princeton University Press/Bollingen, 1998.

Godwin, Gail. *Heart.* New York: William Morrow, 2001.

Lorber, Jacob. *The Great Gospel of John.* Salt Lake City: Merkur Press, 1984.

Mindell, Arnold. *The Quantum Mind and Healing.* Charlottesville, Virginia: Hampton Roads Publishing, 2004.

Picard, Max. *The World of Silence.* Witchita, Kansas: Eighth Day Press, 2002.

Young, Louisa. *The Book of the Heart.* New York: Doubleday, 2003.

THE SCHOOL OF
SPIRITUAL PSYCHOLOGY

A Center for Creative Service

THE SCHOOL OF SPIRITUAL PSYCHOLOGY is a center of learning and research designed to benefit society as a whole by fostering care for soul and spirit in individual life in conjunction with the renewal of culture as the meeting point between the human heart and the world. This enterprise focuses on more than technical training, intellectual comprehension, or individual inner development of a private nature. The programs and activities of the School serve the formation of capacities for consciously experiencing qualities of soul and spirit in oneself, in the profession and work one practices, in home life, community, and in the larger world. The School has been in operation since 1992 and serves people from all walks of life. In 2004, the School moved to a new center in Benson, North Carolina, near Raleigh. The School operates a program in SACRED SERVICE, a program in SPIRIT HEALING, and CARITAS: CARING FOR THOSE WHO HAVE DIED. The School's website is *www.spiritualschool.org*. The School also publishes a semiannual online journal that can be found at *www. sophiajournal.org*.